Flowing from much prayer, thought, and study is this inspiring book by Father David Tickerhoof, tor, on the role of Merciful Penitents in the Renewal and Reform of the Church. Evangelizing Catholic Culture in considering the history of Penitential Movements, the place of the Charismatic Renewal, and other spiritual movements makes a place — a plea — really for Merciful Penitents to foster personal evangelization and disciples of Christ. The Power of the Cross, and Divine Mercy acting in the hearts of the Penitents can enable healing, renewal and atonement in the heart of the Church. This book is recommended as a valuable source for those concerned with spiritual renewal in the Church.

— *Father Daniel Sinisi, tor*

Those who desire to see the power of the Holy Spirit that was present in the early Church become present in our time will find the book informative. The author addresses that those spiritual realities powerfully visible in the early Church that at present have taken a back seat, but if brought to the fore could help bring about renewal in the Church. Another area of the book that I found helpful, as we struggle for ways to renew the Church, is the discussion on the five models of the Church, two that are most familiar and very emphasized, *the institutional and sacramental models*. The other three, *mystical communion, proclamation, and servant models* could broaden and deepen our understanding of the nature and life of the Church.

— *Ruthayn Tickerhoof*

Those of us actively engaged in the New Evangelization know how difficult it can be to find resources that offer a Jesus-centered vision for the formation of missionary disciples, and that breathe Ecclesial Communion. With one ear "to the Holy Spirit" and the other ear "to the Culture", Father David Tickerhoof offers the Church this powerful resource for any Catholic who desires for the Lord Jesus to strengthen and deepen their Baptismal participation in His reconciling mission. Firmly rooted in the Church's spiritual, pastoral, and theological tradition, Evangelizing Catholic Culture is a welcome gift to persons, parishes, and Dioceses wondering how to fruitfully respond to Jesus' call to discipleship today.

— *Sister Maria Kolbe Zamora, Order of Saint Francis (OSF)*

Upon reading this book, I was deeply inspired, convicted, and challenged to become a missionary servant of atonement. In a world and Church beset by radical secularism, Fr. Tickerhoof's discussion and encouragement for missionary servants of atonement seems most timely. The need to remove blockages, unhealed areas in our lives, in order to truly evangelize and/or become servants of mercy, is thoroughly discussed. All of Father Tickerhoof's thoughts are enveloped in the Scriptures and bring those words to life. This book will make a great addition to the reading of those in Pastoral ministry, those anticipating to do ministry, and those seriously pursuing to grow in holiness.

— *Sister Miriam Shindelar,*
The Oblate Sisters of the Blessed Sacrament (OSBS)

Evangelizing
Catholic Culture
New Vision For The New Creation

By Father David Tickerhoof, tor

Evangelization & Holiness New vision for The New Creation

© 2019 by Father David Tickerhoof, tor
ISBN 978-1-073353-68-2

Printed in the United States of America
Author Consultant: Felice Gerwitz, Media Angels
Cover and Layout: Bob Ahrens

For those who have lost hope in
Christ and the Church.

Part III

Introduction

The end of the Jubilee Year of Mercy, 2016, has become the launching pad for a whole new season of Mercy. Already there are several grace-filled opportunities which have been initiated in the life of the Church[1]. This book presents a vision and guiding principles in relationship to this expanded season of Mercy. Its primary goal is to explain the amazing graces available to the faithful of the post-modern age. Realized by few and understood by even fewer is this hidden "way of life," a treasure which will call to those seeking deeper meaning in their lives and provide them with the tools for true evangelization. I call this season the Church's Grace of the Renewal and reform, and its participants Penitents of Merciful Intercession and Atonement. Merciful Penitents are those who live an evangelical life of prayer while offering themselves generously in sacrificial love for others.

We will discuss:
1. A detailed evaluation of the Catholic Church's Grace of the Renewal and reform.

1　　There are very good programs such as Alpha, Christ Life, Light of the World, Christ Renews His Parish.

2. An opportunity to learn to pray with others for specific needs in their life situation.
3. Growth in the ability to do faith-sharing in person-to-person evangelization.
4. How to participate in small-group fellowships which provides the opportunity to experience the joy of relating and making the journey of life together.
5. Ideas for practical service relating to the spiritual and corporal works of mercy.
6. A welcome invitation to our brothers and sisters from other Christian backgrounds to participate in fellowships focused on mercy.

By the mercy of God, for fifty years I have served in the Catholic Church, and with brothers and sisters who belong to other Christian churches and groups. I consider it a privilege to have met and served with individuals who live a merciful penitential life, although they may not identify it in those terms. So, in a sense these individuals are part of a diffusive movement of abundant grace and conversion which has been present and active for some time. Therefore, one of the major objectives of this work is to develop a process, principles, and practical applications which will enhance this sorely needed grace-filled movement in this challenging post-modern age.

My prayer is that this book will be an encouragement to anyone seeking a deeper and more meaningful Christian life than what you may be currently experiencing. It may also help Christians who are active in their parishes and congregations, or give focus and direction to Christians who have completed or are currently involved in evangelization programs.

Part I

Chapter One

A Growing Awareness of the Need for Healing

What is our current experience in the Catholic Church since the close of the Second Vatican Council regarding authentic renewal and reform in the spiritual and pastoral life? Many, for various reasons, have drifted into a superficial spiritual life or have gradually become "Catholic secularists". These individuals receive the Sacraments occasionally, but make their daily choices and decisions from a purely secular humanistic mindset. Some of those remaining who have been faithful to a sacramental and devotional life have gradually become distressfully aware of their unhealed pain and brokenness. Some have come to realize that there is an apparent absence of healings seen in the Scriptures. We are living in a Church which has been diminished in spiritual power and numbers. We are currently assaulted by "the spirit of the world" in a negative and sinful sense, particularly in family life. There is a multitude of destructive criticism and resentment toward the Church that is devastating to the unity and harmony which could bring new life in the Body of Christ. Still, many people are experiencing newness of grace for personal holiness and evangelization. We are witnesses to many grace-filled apostolates and activities that are springing forth and giving us plenty of hope.

In the book of Job, Job struggled intensely with very painful things that the Lord allowed Satan to inflict on him. Today we may know family and friends who are suffering from wounds caused by others. Some are suffering because of negative experiences or difficult situations in their own lives. And some have slipped into a profound apathy and indifference in matters of God and faith. Most of us know people who are suffering from wounds that eventually lead to broken hearts, painful relationships, and disordered lives. Even in our own life we may feel the pain of the absence of forgiveness, emotional wounds, or negative spiritual conditions in varying degrees. The roots of our personal sinfulness are deep in our fallen human personhood.

Luke's Gospel presents the four basic ministries established by Jesus: preaching, teaching, healing, and the casting out of evil spirits. In the beginning of Jesus' ministry at Capernaum, He heals Peter's mother-in-law from a fever. She immediately arises and begins to serve everyone. When the townsfolk want Jesus to stay around and heal others, He tells His disciples that He must go to other towns and proclaim the Good News of the reign of the Kingdom of God. He increasingly reveals his divine power by freeing people from evil spirits, working miracles, and performing other types of healing. Jesus is doing the same works in our world today for those who are open to respond to Him.

Chapter Two

The Role of the Sacraments and the Charism of Healing

An attitude of gratitude surely arises in our hearts when we reflect on the rich grace-filled sacramental life in the Church. The saving power of Jesus' love works magnanimously in all the sacraments. All seven of the sacraments manifest the kind of healing that directly relates to our salvation through faith in Jesus Christ. However, three of them are more directly and specifically geared to healing in our lives. The Eucharist is the source and origin of all healing. The Anointing of the Sick brings physical healing accompanied by emotional and spiritual healing. The Sacrament of Reconciliation brings us healing as we give and receive forgiveness for our sins and renounce the negative effects that they have had in our lives. When we forgive others who have hurt us, we can literally experience healing and freedom within us.

In the Church, these three sacraments of healing are true encounters with Jesus and the primary way we receive healing. At the same time, they cause a wonderful growth in "purity of heart" which draws us more fully into a dynamic union with God. The Sacrament of the Eucharist is the core and all-embracive experience of grace and our essential encounter with Christ's healing power. Fr. Lorenzo Scupoli, a 17th century spiritual writer, illustrates this point beautifully as he described the Eucharist as touching Him.

> *"You reveal the radiance of your love for me, namely that you desire to give me the whole of yourself as food and drink for no other purpose but to transmute the whole of me into yourself... through this union of love, I become as you are: through the union of my earthly heart with your heavenly heart a single divine heart is created in me. Such thought cannot but fill you with wonder and joy. You see yourself so highly valued by God, and so beloved by him. Every favor coming from God's love for you can produce this effect in your soul: but this effect is most natural if you look with understanding on the most Blessed Sacrament of the divine Eucharist."[2]*

In regard to the practice of praying with individuals for spiritual healing, there is a direct relationship between an encounter for healing with the glorified Christ in the Sacraments and the practice of the charism of healing as identified in 1 Corinthians 12:9. However, the two dimensions of healing are distinct in their relationship with each other. I am not in favor of advertising that next week we are going to hold a "healing Mass." The reason for this is that it can easily lead to confusion in the minds of people. Every Eucharistic Liturgy is

2   *Magnificat*, Feb. 1916, p. 134, Fr. Lorenzo Scupoli

a healing Mass! The substantial grace received in the Eucharist is for healing unto Salvation that flows from our immersion in the "Eternal Now" of the death and resurrection of Jesus, in which we actively participate at every Liturgy. The more accurate way for understand healing within a Eucharistic Liturgy is to say, "We will celebrate a Mass next week at which time within the liturgy we will exercise the charism of pastoral healing and pray with individuals for personal healing in their lives."

‹❀Chapter Three❀›

The Charism of Healing in First Corinthians Twelve

Without downplaying the foundational healing ministry of the sacraments, an additional dimension of healing must be highlighted. This gift or charism of healing is identified in the Gospel and in the Catholic Church, but has been sorely ignored or neglected in the daily experience of its members. This gift should be renewed in the contemporary Church, and better understood. Jesus himself consistently used the "charism of healing" exercised by the power of the Spirit in his ministry to others.

When we review the evangelical ministry of Jesus, it is evident that Jesus himself is the model for exercising the pastoral ministry and the gift of the charism of healing we find identified in 1 Corinthians 12:9. If we extract all the healing moments of Jesus in the four Gospels and analyze them, we will clearly come to the conclusion that Jesus used a wonderful integrated method which was both spiritual and rooted in the nature of human development. The healings that Jesus did, for the most part, were always connected to his evangelization, his efforts to build the Kingdom of God.

When we pray with people outside the sacraments, we should also keep evangelization in mind if it seems appropriate, and be willing to speak to the recipient about growing in the Christian life.

Shortly after the Council, Francis McNutt, in his work on inner healing and deliverance, opened the door to an enlightened appreciation of the healing power of Jesus beyond the arena of our Sacramental system. Francis and Judy McNutt centered their healing ministry on training individuals to minister to others in inner healing. The late Fr. Michael Scanlan contributed a little work entitled *Inner Healing*, then with co-author Randy Cirner he wrote a sequel entitled *Deliverance*, reflecting on becoming free from demonic influence. Fr. Bob DeGrandis, SJ specialized in the areas of physical healing and the healing of memories. And most recently, Fr. Richard McAlear, OMI explains prayer for healing in the life of Catholics in his little work entitled, *The Power of Healing Prayer: Overcoming Emotional and Psychological Blocks*. This work gives a very basic and sound summary of the pastoral reality of inner healing in the Church.

Presently, we may be challenged by the work of Fr. Yozefu-B. Ssemakula called *The Healing of Families*. He relates that much human woundedness finds its source in the most intimate societal relationship, the family. He maintains that in these primary relationships, the impact of sin and the manifestation of the power of personal evil contributes to an environment of heaviness, oppression, and darkness which can inhibit the spiritual freedom intended by the Lord for family life. Father's explanation of the consequences of sin and its effects, which foster wounds, bondages, demonic oppression and other influences is quite significant. Akin to this would be the efforts of Neal Lozano, in his book, entitled *Unbound, A Practical Guide to Deliverance*, discussed more extensively below.

Beyond the visible confines of the Catholic Church, Dr. Ed Smith, a Baptist family counselor, presents us with an approach to prayer guiding the participant in the renewal of the mind, and is entitled *Transformation Prayer*. This method goes to the source and origin of our deepest pain. This pain is caused by our negative, untruthful, and unconscious thinking rooted in the depths of our mind. Dr. Smith has designed an in-depth model for mind renewal which generates healing as a by-product of the renewal of the mind. A method of *Transformation Prayer* in the Church has been successfully used in the Sioux Falls Diocese by Mike Snyder and Jane Barz. The name of the ministry is Saint Matthew's Catholic Healing Ministry.

Another very sound and important ministry developed by Dr. Charles Kraft, who has a ministry center to train people in inner healing, which basically is becoming an instrument of God. His most recent work is entitled *Two Hours to Freedom*, which describes his integrated approach to deep level healing. Much of his inner healing ministry would be similar to the other ministries mentioned above. However, he describes for us two unique features which stand out in his approach. The first is that the majority of individuals only need two hours to receive the healing they need, and don't usually return for another session. His main concentration is a focus on praying with individuals starting from the moment of conception, taking into consideration hereditary factors, to gestation and initial moments of infancy. I know of individuals who have received a great deal of healing, but still needed this unique concentration. I believe his approach is very sound. Dr. Kraft uses the example of garbage left in the basement. He states, that where the garbage is, the rats gather, referring to a person's vulnerability to infestation of personal evil. When you get rid of the garbage, the various wounds of the mind, heart and spirit, the rats go, meaning demonic influence. However, evil spirits may need a little help from the individual and the ministers, yet go easily.

After studying all the above approaches to inner healing and recognizing that many people have availed themselves of opportunities to receive inner healing, I think some people still experience a broken heart. I believe some individuals still need to be given attention to the fact that they are still carrying a broken heart because of painful experiences in their lives, and unjust hurts received by others, e.g. painful divorces. But not all pain in the heart needs healing. There exists in the tradition of the Church, an understanding of various degrees of emotional and spiritual pain identifying with the pain in the heart of Jesus unto the love-union as a gift from above.

The approach to healing and deliverance which seems to fit best within the ambit of the Catholic Church is the ministry developed by Neal and Janet Lozano entitled *Unbound Ministry*. It consists in a similar approach as some others mentioned above; however, it operates from a position of "non-confrontational" deliverance. One doesn't fight with evil spirits, but ministers love to the recipient. In short, it is a method of evangelization that provides deliverance from personal evil and aids the recipient in receiving spiritual healing.

In the Lozanos' approach, they employ five keys to spiritual freedom:

1. Standing in the truth of faith and life-giving repentance.
2. Seeking forgiveness of God, others, and most importantly self.
3. Acknowledging and renouncing in the name of Jesus entities of pride, fear, abandonment, the occult etc.
4. Taking authority in the name of Jesus over these spirits or attitudes and commanding them to leave.

5. Finally, praying with the recipient for the Father's love and blessing. This blessing confers a prayer for the recipient in which he or she experiences being a beloved son or daughter of the Father and especially loved by him.[3]

Those who have made significant contributions to healing and freeing individuals from personal evil in pastoral situations are many since the close of Vatican Council II. In addition to the healing identified in the sacramental system of the Catholic Church, these various approaches are drawn from the descriptions of the healing of Jesus in the Gospels, and give direct acknowledgment to the special healing in the Spirit mentioned in 1 Corinthians 12:9, a charism for healing. These authors have studied and practiced in related but different areas in their ministry. In their writings, each of them considers the same realities, but the emphasis of each differs based on the sensitivities and individual needs of those being healed. There is a significant overlap, which can be expected.

Healing is in practice one integral and all-encompassing pastoral ministry which considers an individual's complete life situation. The structural integrity of inner or deep-level healing includes healing from the "world of darkness" and its influences and brings about the cleansing, purifying, and transforming action of the Lord's love. The action of Jesus operating in the power of the Spirit brings spiritual healing to a person's wounds, hurts, and oppressions and gives us a clear appreciation of the healing of the whole person.

The Scriptures present abundant examples of the freedom that Jesus, who is our healer and deliverer, brings about in our life. It is also necessary to ask the Lord to give wisdom and direction and use his power to directly relate to the identified areas where the wounds and hurts of our brothers and sisters

---

3   *Unbound and Unbound Ministry Guide Book* by Neal Lozano

exist, and to rely at all times on the guidance of the Holy Spirit to enlighten and give to ministers the necessary direction.

Infestation or oppression can happen in a number of ways: by absence of forgiveness, childhood trauma, by direct invitation in the practice of the occult, by experiencing painful and serious disorders, by living a sinful and worldly life, by foolish and attentive presence to obviously evil people or situations and extended family bondages. For a person who has a significant long-standing anger problem from wounds from self or others, there would normally be personal evil activity attached to the wounds. It would not be difficult, in a ministry that is well-prepared, to switch from praying with an individual for healing to praying for that person's freedom from oppression in the area which would be related to the unhealed wounds. In fact, it would make the healing which the individual receives more complete. This prayer for cleansing should in no way be considered exorcism.

According to the Catholic Encyclopedia, exorcism is "the act of driving out or warding off demons or evil spirits from persons, places, or things that are, or are believed to be, possessed or under bondage by them or liable to become victims or instruments of their malice. According to Catholic belief, demons are fallen angels who have rebelled against God. Excluded from friendship with God, they retain nevertheless their natural power of acting upon men and the material universe for their own purposes. This power is limited by Divine Providence, but it has been given wider scope in consequence of the sin of humankind. Exorcism is nothing more than a prayer to God, sometimes made publicly in the name of the Church, sometimes made privately to restrain the power of the demons over men and things."[4]

From the Catholic point of view then, there are specific things which occur with a person which can lead to the

---

4   *Catholic Encyclopedia*, vol. 5, p. 748

discernment and decision by competent and well trained individuals, when a particular individual needs formal exorcism. According to the teaching and practice of the Catholic Church, how then may a true case of possession be detected? Always keep in mind that we are also dealing with a whole new science which relates to neurasthenic or psychological personality disorders which can run a hidden parallel in the individual which we think may need formal exorcism. We should always question this in such cases.

Spirits and demons are capable of penetrating and manipulating matter of any sort and can attach, infest, or harass human persons. Hence, according to Saints Thomas and Bonaventure, what occurs in the instance of possession is that a demon enters a human body, the faculties (physical) of which he proceeds to control. The soul, however, cannot be entered or overcome and thus remains free, though its functions with respect to the body operate, as it were, in a suspended fashion. Another theologian mentions that demons are like motors within the bodies which they reside, but in such a way that they do not impress a new quality or a new state of being or constitute with that person a single being.

Some would say that when a person has certain indications, he may be possessed. An individual may have serious spastic movements or hysterical convulsions, but they are not to be considered in any way decisive. The true criterion is the knowledge of secret things, and the possession of languages which were never learned, not to be confused with the charismatic gift of praying in tongues. However, we need to be careful because of our knowledge today of the very real possibility of telepathic communication between individuals. All writers on this matter insist that if the person who seems to be possessed lacks memory as to what he or she did during the seizure, that this would constitute another sure criterion.

Possession, in other words, precludes normal human consciousness. If there are two or more personalities within a person that are not conscious of each other, it is a good indication that we are dealing with possession. This reality would need to be very clear, and should not be confused with what psychology describes as multiple personality disorder or **alters** which are not demons at all. **Alters** in a human personality are usually conscious of each other. However, those who are experienced in formal exorcism say that the only way to tell if a person is possessed is by doing the exorcism. This approach could be significantly problematic. Experts who identify the type of possession which needs formal exorcism say that this degree of possession is rare. This ministry can only be done with the Bishop's appointment and by those he identifies to do the ministry.

In the New Testament, the concept of demons and unclean spirits causing people physical harm is not stressed. The New Testament is primarily concerned with the moral aspect of demons as hostile to man's spiritual good, and Christ's power to overcome the physical harm that demons can do is symbolic of his conquest of spiritual evil and his establishment of the kingdom of God[5]. Acknowledging the reality of demonic possession, Jesus drove demons out of their victims, not by collusion with Beelzebub, the prince of devils, but by the finger of God. Christ also empowered the Apostles and disciples to cast out demons in his name. He transmitted this same power to all believers potentially by *virtue of their Baptism*, but the exercise of this power was subject to certain conditions, namely, prayer and fasting and the careful discernment by appropriate church leaders.

The Acts of the Apostles records how Paul drove out a divining spirit from a girl who brought her masters much

---

5   See Ibid., p. 754

profit by soothsaying. No doubt the other Apostles exercised this power too.[6]

Young men studying for the priesthood in the Catholic Church before Ordination receive a minor order entitled the Order of Exorcist. This means that they are given special anointing and power by Jesus Christ within the Church to take authority over various expressions of personal evil attempting to harm the lay faithful on their spiritual journey. Most of us receiving this Order never give it a second thought when the rite is completed. Therefore, we did not realize that we had been ordained to pray with others for cleansing and healing.

The healing and deliverance ministry is one which is all about love. It is very important that the recipient of ministry really experiences the healing love of God and the love and care of the brothers and sisters who are doing the prayer ministry. The gospel story that characterizes a prayer ministry session is the one of the Good Samaritan, which we all know is one of practical, unconditional love. A prayer ministry session is all about what Jesus is accomplishing in the moment by the power and action of the Holy Spirit. Therefore, those doing the prayer are constantly looking to the Holy Spirit for discernment, guidance, and direction. It is important to realize that the recipient of prayer may be a spiritually wounded, fearful, and struggling individual who needs plenty of care, assurance, and affirmation.

---

6   See Ibid., p. 753

 Chapter Four

A More Recent Gift of the Holy Spirit

As is always true, today a wonderful, powerful, yet gentle gift of the Holy Spirit is being poured out on the whole Church, on all Christian believers, and on many others. From a theological point of view, we could identify it as an actual grace from the Holy Spirit for the purpose of spiritual renewal and pastoral reform, particularly in the Catholic Church. I have frequently used the term **The Church's Grace of the Renewal**. This grace has been received by many with open hearts and with joy. It has brought wonderful change in the lives of many, both internally and externally, responsible for Christian conversion and fruitful works and projects. This grace, by God's beautiful mercy, has taken many concrete expressions with various degrees of intensity. **The Church's Grace of the Renewal** is a process of grace actualized by the Spirit through the power of the Cross and by the experience of the graces and new life of the Resurrection. The dynamism of this gift is rooted in the empowerment and experience of the Paschal Mystery. Many in the Catholic Church are now being invited by the Lord to participate to some degree in this wonderful gift of spiritual refreshment. Yet keep in mind that this new wine is going to need new wine skins.

For the sake of a better understanding, how can we describe gifts or charisms? A charism is an essential gift which informs our call to holiness, ministry, or mission. Charism is a gift given by the Spirit empowering us to share in Christ's mission for the building up of the Body of Christ. This is the term used for special graces which St. Paul describes in 1 Corinthians 12:10 and other places in Scripture. This term is also used to describe a special gift set which identifies the unique grace(s) which empowers a religious community or a special fellowship group. Since this gift set finds its source in the Divine, its initial expression and on-going power is most fundamental to a specific group's spiritual configuration. Charisms are recognized by people and members of a specific group or community that something special beyond human talent and spiritual experience is in operation. There is a sense of the supernatural when a particular charism is significantly operative. This is uniquely the case in relationship to the charism of pastoral healing listed in 1 Corinthians 12:4-10, *"To another the gifts of healing by the one Spirit."*

An insightful approach and adaption to the ministry of healing is what we see Jesus doing in the Scripture. It promotes opportunities for the lay faithful to receive the benefits of this special gift of healing. The door is open to invite those who have a need to respond. It seems that many individuals who make use of the Sacraments receive wonderful and abundant graces. Yet sometimes it is evident that some individuals are not released from painful effects and the consequences of hurts and rejections heaped on them by others or from the devastating byproduct of personal sin - their lives anguished by destructive behaviors and choices. Following Jesus' example, under the inspirations of the Spirit, using the anointing of the charismatic gift of healing could produce wonderful results in the life of the Church.

Why did Jesus perform healings? *"As the Father has loved me, so I have loved you. Live on in my love,"* (John 15:9). Jesus is our Savior and Redeemer! God is love and Jesus is the revelation of the Father's being; He is the Incarnate Love of God made man that brings about our Salvation. Divine healing is the power of God's love in action for the purposes of our human well-being and of achieving our Salvation.

The gift of healing focuses on three dimensions of the human person:
1. The transformation of the mind which reveals enlightened truth.
2. Health, wholeness, and maturity in the human person.
3. The spiritual maturity which empowers individuals to serve with generosity.

When Jesus was moved with pity, He healed to express His compassion. The healing of the widow's dead son is an example of His mercy. Jesus commanded, *"Young man I bid you get up. The dead man sat up and began to speak"* (Luke 7:14-15). In Mark 1, He healed the leper for the same reason, and then the leper made it difficult for Jesus to come into the town, because he proclaimed the healing he received in every location. Jesus healed to lead others to come to faith in him, and to believe that the power and authority he possessed was from God. When Jesus saw their faith, he said to the paralyzed man, *"Child your sins are forgiven." Then a few moments later because of the objections of the Scribes, Jesus said, that you may know that the Son of Man has authority to forgive sins on earth he said to the paralytic, I say to you rise pick up your mat and go home. He rose, picked up his mat at once, and went away in the sight of everyone"* (Mark 2:5-12). When a person has faith, Jesus will gladly heal. When speaking of the centurion's faith,

21

recall the story in Luke when the Jewish leaders ask Jesus to heal the centurion's servant. Jesus said, *"I tell you, I have never found so much faith among the Israelites. When they returned to the house they found the servant in perfect health"* (Luke. 7:9-10).

Jesus healed so people could be free to serve; Jesus healed Peter's mother-in-law, *"and she immediately got up and began to serve"* (Luke. 4:39). Jesus healed and delivered from personal evil; remember the Gerasene demoniac who used to break chains and the demons would drive him into places of solitude. After Jesus cast out the demons, sending them into swine, the townsfolk came out to see what had happened. *"They found the man from whom the devils had departed sitting at His feet dressed and in his full senses"* (Luke 8: 35). Another time, Jesus said that some healing is more difficult. Referring to a boy who had epileptic seizures, *"Jesus told his disciples, this kind can only be driven out by prayer and fasting"* (Mark. 9:29).

All of these manifestations of Jesus's power were signs and wonders to demonstrate the presence of the Kingdom of God, and they happened in order to establish the Kingdom of God on earth. These signs demonstrate Jesus' power and authority, and every bit of this power and authority has been given to the Church. Therefore, the Church needs to be exercising this power and authority magnanimously in the daily life of the Church and in the lives of its members.

The Grace of the Renewal in the Church begins a season of a new life-giving repentance, conversion, change and empowerment for works and witnessing to others about the Good News. However, this experience is not just one of a deep feeling of peace, joy and love. It also activates the power of the Spirit, the tremendous power of the Cross of Jesus, and the power of the glorious resurrection of Jesus. This grace is not three things. **It is one reality in the life of a person!** This reality is crucial in this time of renewal and reform in the contemporary life of the Church. The on-going operation of this threefold power is of importance for one's growth in Christian holiness, and for the practical application of using the charism of healing. It also embraces evangelical witnessing by faith sharing with others, which is witnessing to the Resurrection of Jesus and witnessing to its on-going power in the lives of individuals in the life of the Church.

Our attachment to sin in our life can effectively block blessings, healings and charismatic gifts the Lord desires us to receive in order to evangelize and build the Kingdom of God. Sin leads us into spiritual darkness and bondage, which prevents us from seeing the light and glory of God in our minds and hearts. So in Romans 3:23, St. Paul reminds us, *"we have all sinned and are deprived of God's glory."*

Awhile back I was browsing the used book section at a local bookstore in Bradenton, Florida, when I came across a paperback entitled *Loving God* by Charles Colson. Chapter Nine recounts the story of the famous gangster Mickey Cohen, who at that time ruled the underworld in California[7]. Mickey died of cancer in 1976. By this time Billy Graham had become a very famous evangelist. Several of Mickey's henchmen had become Christian and were in the process of making big changes in their lives. This experience of men that Mickey knew well aroused a genuine interest in him in regard to the Christian way of life, and he made a concerted effort to contact Billy Graham. However, in the end he was not able to give himself over to becoming a Christian. In one instance, Billy sensed a strong resistance in Mickey. Why was this so? As Mickey began to open the door to the ideas of Christianity, he discovered that doing so involved a significant choice. He must totally surrender himself or close the door. When he finally understood what was demanded of him, what repentance meant, he closed the door. Mickey would not repent. When pushed on the point he answered: "What is wrong with being

7   *Loving God* by Charles Colson, Chap. 9

a Christian gangster?" At heart each one of us has to relate to the same reality. We are sinners and struggle with repentance. Many of us may be the Christianized versions of the sinners that we already are, and are determined to remain without repentance and conversion. We cannot love God and remain what we are. We must repent, and be willing to eventually surrender our total self and give our whole life to the Lord and his plan for us.

The biblical word for repentance is *metanoia*. It literally means a change of mind. It can be described as a mighty change in mind, heart, and life, brought about by the transforming work of the Spirit of God. Thus, repentance is replete with radical implications for a fundamental change of mind which not only turns us from a sinful past, but transforms our life plan, values, ethics, and actions as we begin to see the world through God's eyes rather than ours. That kind of transformation requires the ultimate surrender of self. Repentance is the keynote of the Gospel. The first public words of Jesus in the Gospel of Mark presents the call for repentance, *"Repent and believe the Good News."* (Mark. 1:15). Repentance is the inescapable consequence of regeneration, the cause to be renewed, restored, and to be spiritually reborn. It is an essential part of the conversion process that takes place under the convicting power of the Holy Spirit. But life-giving repentance is also a continuing state of mind and heart. Without continual repentance, Christian growth is very slow, and loving God is more difficult than it needs to be. With this understanding one is able to see why the **Grace of the Renewal**, that is abundantly available in the life of the Church, becomes very important for each Christian. It entails a release of the power and gifts of the Holy Spirit in a manner which sets in operation a **life-giving repentance** which opens a new door to grace and fuels the continual process that Charles Colson describes in his book.

The Good News or the Gospel is the power of our salvation. The heart of the Gospel is Jesus Christ. Life giving repentance flows from a personal relationship with Jesus who is our Lord and Savior. It is in His merciful love that we receive the power to overcome the obstacles which hinder a love-union with our Lord and our brothers and sisters. In our society, the opposing style of life is termed radical secularism which is a movement or a cultural experience which destroys a person's or a people's mind by a corruption of truth. It is a warping of a human person's spirit and causes a loss of the meaning of life, as well as an obliteration of true religion by neutralizing God and by removing His presence and activity from human existence. It is a subtle but a drastic violation of human and religious freedom, and can use various methods such as force, political action, or legislation to achieve its goals. Like a cancer it spreads its noxious growth through various forms of religious indifferentism. As a movement it demands the right to acquire pleasure quickly and fosters the spirit of the world in a negative sense. It induces a lack of attraction toward spiritual things, a laziness which is willing to remove the experience of God from society while dissociating from the obligation of responding to the experience and presence of God's activity and expectations. Thus, it opens the door to the influence of sin, a worldly spirit, and demonic manipulation.

The answer lies within each of us, both good and evil primarily passing through the human heart, but to find it we must come face to face with who we really are. This is a difficult process which can only happen by the Lord's rich and powerful mercy and grace. The hidden and false self is buried deep within our hearts; confronting our false self is a very painful project. Any person who has made a serious decision for conversion can give testimony to that reality. When we finally realize the horrific reality of sin within us, we can be tempted to despair. But the good God has provided a way for us to be freed from the evil that is within; it is through the door of life-giving repentance and conversion leading to reconciliation, in which our minds and hearts are changed. When we truly comprehend our own nature, repentance is no frightening message, no morbid idea for self-flagellation. It is, as the early Church Fathers said, a gift God grants which leads to life. Life-giving repentance is a powerful gift of the Spirit of Love. It is the key to the door of spiritual liberation, to the only real freedom we can ever know. This process consists in embracing the wisdom, power, and the glory of the Cross of the Crucified One, which releases the enlightened power and life of the Resurrection in an individual's life. This experience of grace is the love of God operating as the **Grace of the Renewal**. The three-fold power of the Spirit, the Cross, and the Resurrection operate as one reality within a person, and brings a new transforming life within the soul of a committed Christian.

God bestows His graces in abundance in many ways, and somewhat differently to each individual as He chooses. Therefore, we might ask, what are some of the observable features that individuals experience in receiving these renewal graces? Generally, within this process of change and conversion one can become much more aware of the presence, operation, and power of the Holy Spirit in one's life. Sometimes difficult burdens and pressures are released, and a more open and conscious love of God and others can develop. After receiving these actual graces an individual tends to be more attracted to spiritual things and wants to develop a more consistent personal prayer life. Frequently accompanying this **Grace of the Renewal** is an enhanced appreciation and operation of the various gifts of the Spirit we find in the Scriptures. This experience may lead one to focus on God's promise in Ezekiel, *"I will give them a new heart and put a new spirit within them; I will remove their stony heart from their bodies, and replace* *it with a natural heart"* (Ezekiel 11:19). The **Grace of the Renewal** is a gift of the Lord given to the Church of our time. It can be viewed as a door open to a wonderful journey of grace and conversion, a process of personal transformation.

The Sacraments together with the charismatic gift of pastoral healing serve to generously provide various opportunities for individuals to receive the magnificent and wonderful healing graces operating in the Catholic Church at the turn of this century. It comes down to making a decision to be open to receive a new fresh spiritual way of thinking. *"And be renewed in the spirit of our minds, and put on the new self, created in God's way in righteous and holiness of truth"* (Ephesians 4:23-24). The **Grace of the Renewal**, that fountain of Holy Spirit living, is available to anyone who is significantly yearning for more in the spiritual life. It is for those who have the feeling there is something important missing in their spiritual life or those who know that they have lost in a significant degree intimacy in the experience of prayer. They should begin praying to the Lord to receive the experience of the **Grace of the Renewal**. This grace is not just for those who have little or no personal relationship with the Lord, or who have stopped participating in the organizational life of the Church. The **Grace of the Renewal** is also for Catholics who are weekly churchgoers, but who live the rest of the week with a secular humanistic way of thinking. These individuals may not have much of a daily prayer life, and would not understand what it means to walk with the Lord by bringing His presence into every circumstance or decision during the day. If the knowledge and experience of living in the Lord is not at the heart of my life, then I am a Catholic who needs some degree of empowerment in the life changing gift of the **Grace of the Renewal.**

"Every tree that is not fruitful will be cut down and thrown into the fire. I baptize you in water for the sake of reform, but the one who will follow me is more powerful than I. I am not even fit to carry his sandals. He will baptize you in the Holy Spirit and fire" (Matthew. 3:10-11).

Chapter Five

The Grace of the Renewal and the Value of Suffering

Highlighting the notion of fire, the **Grace of the Renewal** as an actual grace and a spiritual gift of God's love, which can be actualized by the experience of suffering. However, it also needs an accompanying surrender and commitment by an individual in order for it to become transforming. Heather King discusses this point in her meditations on Elizabeth Leseuer in the Magnificat prayer book[8]. Elizabeth records in her journal a deep experience of conversion in Rome while kneeling at the tomb of St. Peter. This experience plus the suffering she subsequently endured in her life invited her to a deeper exploration of her own faith, until then a rather conventional faith. All the while she continued to develop a rich and hidden interior life. "Has my life known any unhappier time than this?" She is referring to the various forms of suffering and desolation she experienced. "And yet through all these trials and in spite of a lack of interior joy, there is a deep place that all these waves of sorrow cannot touch. "There I can feel how completely one with God I am, and I regain strength and serenity in the heart of Christ." Elizabeth

---

8   *Magnificat*, Jan., 2015, pp. 49-51

was uniquely transformed by the suffering she experienced in her life. Her immersion in a love-union with God and the fruitfulness of her life clearly illustrates the characteristics which constitute the **Grace of the Renewal** in relationship to the power of the Cross. Suffering is the highest form of action, the highest expression of the wonderful communion of saints. This suffering is an act of love for others, and advances the great causes that one longs to serve. We witness in Elizabeth's life the full attainment of the **Grace of the Renewal**. Through embracing the Cross of Jesus and its transforming power which brings about the new life of the Resurrection, Elizabeth lived a heroic life of generous prayer and service to others.

Another way of gaining this **Grace of the Renewal** is through a consistent life of prayer, and the daily reading of the Word of God. Yet another way is involvement in compassionate works of mercy or other evangelical services. These works bear great fruit when the individuals doing them have a profound and rich spiritual life. One final way that I might offer is a faithful and generous response to the graces of one's particular calling in life. Rarely would just one of these approaches seeking the **Grace of the Renewal** exist alone, and you may have some things to add to this list as you grow more fully in the release of the Holy Spirit.

◈ Chapter Six ◈
An Approach to Pastoral Ministry

"*Jesus went around to all the towns and villages, teaching in their synagogues, proclaiming the Gospel of the Kingdom, and curing every disease and illness. At the sight of the crowds, his heart was moved with pity for them because they were troubled and abandoned, like sheep without a shepherd. Then he said to his disciples, 'The harvest is abundant but the laborers are few; so ask the master of the harvest to send out laborers for his harvest.' Then he summoned his twelve disciples and gave them authority over unclean spirits to drive them out and to cure sickness and disease of every kind*" (Matthew 9: 35-10: 1).

"*Jesus instructed the twelve, "Go to the lost sheep of the house of Israel. As you go, make this proclamation: 'the Kingdom of heaven is at hand.' Cure the sick, raise the dead, cleanse lepers, and drive out demons. Without cost you have received; without cost you are to give*" (Matthew 10: 6-8).

What is the relationship of the charismatic gift of healing stated in 1 Corinthians 12:9 to the notion of healing in the Sacraments? When the charism of healing in pastoral ministry is the focus, and if the person is Catholic, it may be useful to invite the recipient of the ministry to consider celebrating the appropriate sacrament. Sometimes the celebrating of the sacrament of healing better disposes the person for a more complete pastoral ministry session. This approach may provide a more open readiness for the individual to experience a deeper and more successful pastoral ministry healing session. It is important to note that taking this approach is not always needed or fits the given pastoral situation. Therefore, wise discernment is necessary. Within the context of every healing session it is helpful to share the gospel in relationship to the individual's need.

I want to emphasize the important role of discernment and the gift of the discernment of spirits. Discernment is a gift that accompanies the work of grace in all matters which involve Christian life, ministry, and all circumstances. However, the gift of **discernment of spirits** is a unique charism which enables one to know what spirits are working in a given situation. In the context of a ministry focusing on our relationship to God's immediate guidance, are we dealing with the work of the flesh, the spirit of the world, or the presence and activity of evil spirits or some other kind of personal evil? It is rather obvious that the gift of **discernment of spirits** is essential for any ministry situation. Therefore, those who do pastoral ministry should be very familiar with the nature and operation of this gift, and appreciate that this gift is at the core of any activity in the healing ministry.

⚜Chapter Seven⚜

The Transforming Power of the Cross

In Galatians, St. Paul spells out for us the nature of the reality and power of the Cross in his own personhood. *"I have been crucified with Christ, and the life I live now is not my own; Christ is living in me. I still live my human life, but it is a life of faith in the Son of God, who loved me and gave himself for me. I will not treat God's precious gift as pointless"* (Galatians 2:19b-20a). Then, in the sixth chapter he writes about the same reality in relationship to the world. *"May I never boast of anything but the Cross of our Lord Jesus Christ. Through it, the world has been crucified to me and I to the world"* (Galatians 6:14). *"All that matters is that one is created anew"* (Galatians 6:15b). It can easily be shown in Scripture that the Spirit changes those in whom he comes to dwell. He so transforms them that they begin to live a completely new kind of life. Samuel tells Saul, *"The Spirit of the Lord will take possession of you and you shall be changed into another man"* (1 Samuel 10:6). St. Paul writes, *"As we behold the glory of the Lord with unveiled faces, that glory, which comes from the Lord who is the Spirit transforms us all into his likeness, from one degree of glory to another"* (2 Corinthians 3:18). Does this not show that the Spirit of the Lord changes those in whom he comes to dwell and alters the whole pattern of their lives?[9]

All suffering and evil that exists or that will ever exist in reality is now completely taken up and transformed through the Cross. All human suffering introduces a transforming quality initiated in the divine reality flowing from the risen and glorified Lord Jesus. This reality is at the center of the Catholic theology of salvation, atonement, and reparation. We see this truth modeled in our time by the life of Padre Pio, a recent saint sharing in the divine self-revelation of Jesus. He clearly manifested the full gamut of healing both sacramental and charismatic in his life, ministry, and suffering. The charismatic mystical phenomenon of the wounds of the Crucified manifested in his flesh illustrates for us a complete understanding and perspective in relationship to the transforming mystery of healing centered in the Cross. His transforming union with the Crucified One was the source of his mission, and encompassed atonement to the Father, reparation for sin, celebration of the healing Sacraments, healing the wounds of others, spiritual warfare, the mission of intercession, and finally the building of a medical community. It is a challenge and sometimes hard for us to understand the effective, fruitful and all embracive power available to us through the Cross. Yet in the dynamic of a living Faith these realities highlight the complete picture of healing in the Church.

One of the reasons that some individuals are hesitant about the **charism of healing** lies in the misunderstanding of healing itself. In a certain sense we expect too much from healing. Healing rarely stands alone for its own sake. It is usually in relationship to something else. In the ministry of Jesus, in addition to pure compassion, the healing and

9   *Liturgy of the Hours of the Church*, Vol. III, 7th week of Easter, p.992

miracles he performed were to demonstrate the breaking in of the Kingdom of God. In many instances healing can alleviate some of the wounds derived from others, and relieve pressures from other forms of darkness and infestation of personal evil. But healing is not going to take away all the human deficiencies and imperfections that we have in our lives; and in many instances we will take them to the grave. Thank God for the purifying mercy of Purgatory, as well as the ascetical measures taken to grow in spiritual and human maturity in our lifetime. The fact is that God is quite capable of giving us the grace that is necessary for us to achieve significant degrees of holiness as he works with our human nature.

⟨§⟩ C h a p t e r   E i g h t ⟨§⟩

The Access Points Which Invite the Influence of Personal Evil

Most authors who write about healing and deliverance identify generally four access points which can invite the influence of personal evil. The first area to consider is that of forgiveness and childhood trauma. There may be certain areas in us where un-forgiveness effectively blocks out God's grace, and particularly the grace of healing. It is a consistent and a well-known experience of prayer ministers that when praying for healing in the lives of prayer recipients and a problem is not responding, un-forgiveness is most often at the root.

Somewhat related to the area of un-forgiveness is trauma. Trauma creates a shock to our spirit, at least for a time, and develops a belief system based on lies. It can lead to disorientation and disassociation and causes us to become vulnerable. One's negative self-image, at these times, can profoundly shape our self-concept. The mindset and feelings of self-condemnation, worthlessness, inadequacy, abandonment, and self-rejection can enter a person because of damage done to one's spirit and emotions, which can be easily manipulated by Satan, and thus resentment and un-forgiveness can creep into the inner person, resulting in unhealthy disassociation, hardness of heart, or a debilitating fear that robs us of the goodness of life.

The second access point is unhealthy or sinful relationships. Destructive relationships are not just physical; they are also spiritual. What can be called negative is when the friendship is not enhancing the God-created good in either person, making it an ungodly relationship. This begins to have negative spiritual consequences for those involved, and the liability is experienced as a transfer of spiritual baggage or spiritual negativity between the two people. The negativity is a power that opens the door to sin and the manipulation and the oppression of Satan. This negative spiritual influence is a powerful bondage. We need to keep in mind that once there is sin, there is an expressed invitation, although it may largely be unconscious, made to the evil one to come and inhabit or have an influence in that relationship. This includes all kinds of relationships but especially sexual relationships, pornography and sin (a serious and severe violation of an individual God-given dignity) with the persons viewed.

The third access point is occult involvement. This topic deserves a specific study, but I only mention it here to make us aware of its very negative impact on individuals. Simply put, we put God on an equal footing with not only a simple creature of His, but a creature who in his very rebellion against God, wanted to be like God. It is precisely because we confirm Satan in his being Satan when we turn the glory and honor due to God to him. He can get significant power over us, which is more than ordinary influences of evil. When some in our contemporary Church life ignore, deny, or dissociate from this truth, it is certainly to their detriment and possibly to the detriment of others for whom they may have pastoral responsibility.

The fourth access point is family bondages. The four common areas in which bondages can come into families are circumstances of life, behaviors, diseases, and habits or patterns of difficulty. Look for patterns and identify spiritual, emotional, and physical difficulties that are repeated in our ancestral lines. Just open your eyes to anything in your family, and make note of anything that catches your attention as repeated. Give attention to the existence of adoption in your family. Sometimes the primordial wound of the heart exists in very good adopted persons because of not knowing their parents of origin. You will notice that often you may not be able to find "factual proof" for some of these things; however, the painful and debilitating evidence is expressed in symptomatic behavior. If there is a consistent problem for a long time, it is worthwhile working it down to its roots, through the frequency of repetition. Some issues in healing need to be gradually related to through in-depth un-covering, level by level.

Adding to the four access points, it seems necessary to create a fifth category regarding addictions. In my early years of ministry, the main focus of ministry attention related to the addiction of alcohol through the blessing of the Twelve Step approach. Now in the popular literature of human development and in the wide arena of the social sciences the emphasis seems to have shifted. The primary attention initially given to personality disorders seems to have moved towards the alleviation of the mysterious harm caused by the emergence of a huge number of multiple addictions prevalent in our society. Most experts seem to think that the root cause of addiction is in the mind. However, the emotional upheaval and the spiritual disintegration accompanying cognitive dissonance is also a monumental experience. In recent years in our nation, many are rapidly moving away from a God-centered society. The values and behaviors in the United States are now more infested with the destructive forces of secularism, individualism, and materialism. Most caring people have become significantly more aware of the massive amounts of compulsive destructive addictions and violence in our country and sometimes in their own families. The contemporary forms of asceticism, counseling, and spiritual direction in Catholic life, as good as they are in themselves, have only made a small dent in the cure of addictions experienced painfully by many of our brothers and sisters. One of the reasons why freedom from addictions is so difficult is because of its compulsive nature. Some authors say where there is addiction there is unrighteousness and sin. For our purposes here it is important to note that addictions have become a point of vulnerability and access for the oppression and infestation of personal evil.

It may be well to note that the Unbound Ministry founded by Neal and Janet Lozano provides a format for a successful plan of pastoral healing. In addition to its non-confrontational approach, it also gives significant attention to the area of ancestral healing as well as attention to the whole person. Some of the effects of this ministry of mercy and charity may be helpful for some to experience a deeper freedom from the negative influences in one's own life and immediate family. In addition to the freedom we may experience from this approach to the healing ministry, it teaches us the truth that our on-going freedom and transformation to spiritual freedom and human maturity also entails a struggle with the world, the flesh and the devil. We need to keep our freedom and rejoice in our healing.[10]

Finally, the last dimension in considering healing and deliverance is one that you will not usually find discussed in evaluations of the deliverance and healing ministry; however, we should be very certain that we, as a nation, are reaping the impact, devastation, and wounds from the sinful national and

10   The published and recorded works of Unbound may be found on their website or Amazon.com

social injustice of slavery and the obliteration of the Native American peoples over the past centuries. We seem to have dissociated from the powerful impact on our culture and on the individuals in our culture which we have tolerated. The "peculiar system" of slavery reaching back to the 1600 has embedded the sin of racism, the devastating effects of which still exist to this day. And the genocide of the Native Americans has immensely wounded both the perpetrators and victims. Any length of time spent on a Reservation will demonstrate the truth of this reality. When praying with individuals for ancestral healing it is necessary to pray for deliverance and healing to release the dark and negative effects of oppression for individuals whose extended family bondages carry the weight of our national sin.

The Unbound Ministry configures the framework for a successful plan of personal, pastoral, social healing and deliverance. In light of its non-confrontational approach, it also relates to ancestral healing as well as the other dimensions of the whole person. The secondary effects of this work of mercy and charity result in the experience of a deeper freedom from darkness and oppression in one's own life and immediate family. This type of prayer can be very challenging to some. We easily forget that all the dimensions of this approach to freedom relate to much more than simply being healed from some painful wounds. Our complete spiritual warfare and transformation to human maturity and deliverance involves a struggle with the world, the flesh and the devil. In the practice of spiritual warfare, we have the assurance of the Risen Christ that in him we definitely will be victorious. Please keep in mind that our personal victory exists in the context of the total and complete victory Jesus Christ has won for us.

Part II

Chapter One

Components Necessary for Evangelization
Listening to the Voice of God

It may be useful to consider some things in regard to one's personal relationship to God, which can be important for spiritual maturity and successful approaches to pastoral ministry and personal evangelization. It is common in spiritual literature to read about the necessity of individuals highlighting the reality of *vox Dei*, hearing the voice of God. God speaks to us all the time through Sacred Scripture, liturgy, people, circumstances, events, and in other ways. Some may wonder how to listen to the Lord, to hear the word of the Lord and discern it. God frequently spoke directly to the prophets. And in the New Testament, Jesus speaks about His continual communication with God, and He always listened to the Father before He acted on anything. For example, He went off to the mountain to pray to the Father before He chose his disciples. In the private revelations of particular individuals in the tradition of the Church, God spoke many times to them. So it is very clear that it is God's merciful intention to intimately speak to every baptized disciple of Christ. It is unquestionably essential for those individuals who minister to others to know how to maturely hear the "voice of the Lord", Who personally gives to individuals who desire a relationship with Him guidance, direction, and various forms of inspiration.

"To hear the voice of the Lord" is a natural and supernatural experience, which is important to appreciate and understand for the sake of personal holiness as well as being essential for a prayer ministry. "We have not received the spirit of the world but the Spirit that is from God, so that we may freely understand the things freely given us by God. And we speak about them not with words taught by human wisdom, but with words taught by the Spirit, describing spiritual realities in spiritual terms." (2 Corinthians 2: 12-13) In spiritual terms means: the Spirit teaches spiritual people a new mode of perception, and an appropriate language by which they can share their self-understanding, their knowledge about what God has done in them." *"Now the natural person does not accept what pertains to the Spirit of God, for to him it is foolishness and he cannot understand it, because it is appraised spiritually."* (1 Corinthians 2: 14-15) The spiritual person, however, can evaluate everything, but is not subject to appraisal since spiritual persons have been given knowledge of what pertains to God; they share in God's own capacity, to whom the mind of Christ has been revealed. The natural person is one whose existence, perceptions, and behaviors are determined by purely natural principles and behaviors in the mind and the flesh. Such persons remain on a purely natural level. These individuals in Scripture are called to become spiritual and mature in their perceptions and behaviors.

It is necessary to be open to "hear the voice of the Lord" when praying with others. So then how should we personally try to grasp this notion, especially in pastoral ministry and in Christian service? The context within which we grow and mature in the practice of listening to the Lord is the revealed

Word of God and the inspired teaching of the Church. The reality of the dynamic of relating to the Lord's Word needs to be taught to us, in order that the practical elements of following inspirations in the mind and "words" in the heart may be easily understood by others. Remembering we have been created naturally to communicate with God, and we are gifted by our Baptism to experience the awareness of the presence and movements of grace in our interior life. God is Spirit and Jesus, the Glorified Lord, relates to us in our spirit through His active presence, and through the insights, inspirations, and power of the Holy Spirit. This experience of grace in us is humanly intelligible, though a mystery. What a joy it is to understand that we can practically know the Lord and His active presence in our hearts, our lives, and in our relationships, and thus experience communication with Him.

Awhile back, I was ministering to an elderly woman in a large extended care facility in Bradenton, Florida. I celebrated Reconciliation, gave the Anointing of the Sick and Holy Communion to her. Afterwards she said to me, "you know Father, I know the Lord very well." Then she went on to tell me that she was part of a healing team which prayed for years with people. She recounted with tender joy an incident when the leader of the team asked her to pray for a dying baby and the baby was instantly healed. The great news is that the Lord created us with exterior and interior receptors to be able to receive and understand the movements of the Holy Spirit in our communication with the Divine. For example, if we are walking down the street by ourselves, we would not be surprised to realize that we are talking to ourselves about many things. This is this same interior faculty in which the Holy Spirit is able to infuse and form words in us by His action or work when we give prayerful attention to it. The Saints experienced this phenomenon frequently, and the mystical tradition identifies this mode of communication as "locutions." In short, it is important to acknowledge and desire to be aware of His presence, grow in the awareness of His presence and just begin to communicate with Him, with humble patience and moving forward in our faith, which is the key to grow in courage and love.

In these matters, good counsel and direction protects us from errors. There are multiple ways in which the Lord communicates with us. We can also receive direct revelation in our understanding as well as through various forms of inspiration, including the circumstances of our life, and yes, sometimes even in our dreams. Of course, this communication from the Lord always needs to be tested and discerned; St. John tells us to *"test every spirit"* (1 John 1-3). It is not easy to become good at discerning the word of the Lord. We always need to ask ourselves the question: Is what I believe to be the word of the Lord coming from the Lord, the unredeemed part of me, or from a deception by Satan? The devil is good at mimicking the various communication gifts of the Spirit. St. Paul in Second Corinthians reminds us that Satan presents himself as an "Angel of Light." It takes a great deal of humility and practice to mature in hearing the word of the Lord, and knowing when and how to act on it in a manner that is pleasing to Him. Isaiah instructs us in listening to the Lord, "By waiting and by calm is your salvation; in quiet and trust is your strength" (Isiah 30:15). However, since Jesus alone is the healer, it is reasonable and necessary to know what Jesus is doing in a given pastoral ministry situation. The divine/human interplay in grace through the spiritual activity of conversation, communication, and communion with the Lord, is what we mean by hearing the word of the Lord, listening to it, and discreetly following it as He speaks to us, giving us various forms of guidance and direction in a given situation.

Briefly here are a few things about this wonderful possibility. The first and probably the most fundamental point is that the Lord in His great love desires and has created us to communicate with Him. This dynamic is evident in the story of Adam and Eve in the Garden of Eden. An involved and mature communication with God in our life and ministry presupposes that we walk closely with Him in all the moments of our daily life. Praying always is one way of expressing this reality. Mary is identified in spiritual writings as the **attentive Virgin** who is always open and receptive to Divine communication. Depending on the situation, sometimes the Lord takes the initiative and sometimes we are able to do that. The door to this relationship is a life of prayer. This process is enhanced by an active life in the Holy Spirit, and a practical ability to use the gifts of the Holy Spirit which pertain to what is going on in a given moment or situation, particularly in personal prayer or in a ministry context.

Chapter Two

The Anointing of the Spirit and the Grace of the Renewal

Life from God's Anointing: In the First Letter of St. John we read, *"You have the anointing that comes from the holy one, and you all have knowledge . . . Let what you heard from the beginning remain in you. If what you heard from the beginning remains in you, then you will remain in the Son and in the Father."*

"As for you, this anointing that you received from Him so that you do not need anyone to teach you. But His anointing teaches you about everything and is true and not false; just as it taught you to remain in Him" (1 John 2:24-26).

The anointing of the Spirit that we receive is given, determined, and configures the Apostolic charism. It is the active, dynamic revelation of the Trinitarian life which is Apostolic in nature, and is a gift given by Jesus on the night of the Resurrection and by the coming of the Spirit at Pentecost. The Apostolic charisms derived from these experiences are gifts of empowerment for the building up of the Body of Christ, the Church. This is for every new-born Christian from above. This anointing has many expressions, which are also determined by

God's special work of the moment. The dynamic operation of the anointing is expressed uniquely by the action of God in a given work or situation. The anointing that we have received is not something that is hidden deeply within us in a way that we are rarely aware. It is a part of the dynamic grace life we have received in our water Baptism and Confirmation with the gifts of the Spirit. At times we lose touch with it, and the operation of this wonderful grace is stymied or operates at such a low level that we are not aware of it. Some Christians will say from time to time, I experience God as just a vague presence and somewhat at a distance from my daily choices and situations in my life. Thus, all of a sudden, we come face to face with a need for the empowerment of the **Grace of the Renewal**. In the experience of this grace one becomes alive and sensitive to the moments of God's anointing in events, specific situations, and with particular persons. Before some are able to receive this gift, this actualizing grace, they may need a certain amount of healing, which itself is a special charism of the Spirit that demonstrates a special spiritual authority. We see this in operation in many instances in the life and ministry of Jesus when he performed a healing or deliverance. Anointing is the power of the Spirit which makes our gifts function with ease.

There are various movements which have programs which effectively help people to receive this **Grace of the Renewal**. Each individual is different, and the initial experience of this grace is more effective in some than others. However, some sort of assistance by others through prayer and various programs is usually necessary. This does not mean that the Lord is limited just to these methods, because the Lord is the Spirit and the Spirit blows where He wills.

What are we after here in this notion of the **Grace of the Renewal**? We need to seek after a similar experience that the members of the early Church received when they fully repented from their sins, committed their lives to Jesus as Lord and Savior, and prayed to receive the Holy Spirit. However, at this point we are not speaking about individuals who are not Christian. We are referring to people who have received Christian Baptism and Confirmation or something similar to it. In attempting to describe this reality in a sentence I would say, individuals should seriously prepare to receive what we could term **a re-empowerment of the early Apostolic Grace, a fresh experience of the newness of the full and complete Christian life given as gift by the Holy Spirit.** I would suggest that some sort of a well-planned program is needed to assist in preparing individuals to seek the Lord for this profound grace of inner spiritual refreshment.

My intent here is not to provide a detailed description of a possible approach, but to discuss this matter in relationship to the topic of pastoral healing. Some folks want to stay as far away from the possibility of any healing as they can whether they need it or not. This is understandable because many people have a hard time looking deeply within themselves. Also some individuals who tend to interior reflection abuse this gift by excessive and inordinate introspection. This defect can easily arise from an individual who struggles from a worrisome and fearful attitude to life and spiritual perfection. An unhealthy narcissism may be the root cause. Some well-intentioned people know that they need healing but are filled with fear or a simple ignorance of what to do about it. Others have disassociated from their unhealed wounds or hurts and don't remember them anymore; however, the wounds are still very operative in a negative manner in their personality or character, even though they may experience a certain degree of psychic amnesia. To deal with some of this before receiving the **Grace of the Renewal** augurs for a more profound spiritual experience; however, in the end, it is up to the individual to determine to what degree of preparation he is willing to undergo in regard to an in-depth opportunity.

In early January, we celebrate the greatness of the Holy Name of Jesus. In regard to healing there is nothing more powerful than the Name of Jesus, which is His person, and nothing more cleansing, transforming, and freeing than the Blood of Jesus. When we put together the Name and the Blood, the realms of darkness are dispelled, Satan is defeated, and individuals are delivered and healed from festering wounds and destructive tendencies, and then are able to enjoy living victorious lives.

In the words of Bishop Ignatius Brainchaninov, "After the mystical supper, among other sublime, final commandments and orders, the Lord Jesus Christ instituted prayer by **His name**. He gave this way of prayer as a new, extraordinary gift, a gift of infinite value. The Apostles partly knew already the power of the name of Jesus; they healed incurable diseases by it, they reduced devils to obedience, conquered, bound, and expelled them by it. This most mighty, wonderful name **the Lord orders us to use in prayer**. He promised that such prayer will be particularly effectual. *'Whatever you ask in my name I will do'"* (John14:13). The name of Jesus contains all, and it is the only one that contains the power and presence it signifies, *"For there is no other name under heaven given to the human race by which we are to be saved"* (Acts 4:12).

Chapter Three

The Name of Jesus and the Charism of Healing and Deliverance

In regard to simple deliverance, I would like to make a few comments about using the power and authority of Jesus' name in this type of prayer. In September, 2000, the Vatican issued a document on praying deliverance prayers using the name and the spiritual authority of Jesus. This directive of the Congregation of the Faith, *Instruction on Prayer for Healing*, mentions that under the direct anointing of this prayer, this authority should be reserved to sacerdotal persons. The recipient of the ministry should use the Name of Jesus when receiving deliverance prayer. Lay ministers may do the deliverance prayer, but have the recipient of the prayer do the authoritative renouncing. Leaders of the Church may have a concern in regard to keeping a clear distinction between simple deliverance and formal exorcism. But more than likely the issue is pointing to the fact that the recipients of ministry should be the ones to use their baptismal graces in relationship to receiving healing and renouncing personal evil. Of course this directive pertains only to members of the Catholic Church.

I have personal knowledge of lay ministers who use this grace quite effectively in other Christian denominations.

The Church supports the use of the charismatic gifts. The three most recent Popes, in some of their writings or talks, have directly and clearly invited the members of the Church to accept the charismatic gifts gratefully as gifts from God and to use them. The Vatican Council II endorsed them in the Document on the Church.

> *"Moreover, the Holy Spirit not only sanctifies and guides God's people by the sacraments and the ministries, and enriches it with virtues, he also distributes special graces among the faithful of every state of life, assigning his gifts to each as he chooses. By means of these special gifts he equips them and makes them eager for various activities and responsibilities that benefit the Church in its renewal or its increase, in accordance with the text: to each is given the manifestation of the Spirit for a good purpose. These charisms, the simpler and the more widespread as well as the most outstanding, should be accepted with a sense of gratitude and consolation, since in a very special way they answer and serve the needs of the Church."[11]*

---

11   *Liturgy of the Church*, vol. III, 7th Week of Easter, p. 984

The seven Sacraments, instituted by Christ, totally cover the life situations of the members of the Church. All of them give special grace for the specific areas that they identify. And all of them contain within them the power to bring the change necessary for salvation. So it is accurate to say that each Sacrament contains a healing component in relationship to Salvation. However, this is not the same as the charism of healing articulated in Corinthians. This charism is a unique anointing and action of the Spirit for healing in addition to the Church's sacramental system. Therefore, we could say it is a special pastoral charism in addition to but rooted in our Sacramental Life, and operative in the pastoral realms of the Church and life of its members. Our Sacramental life and the charism of healing flow from the same source, namely, a living encounter with the Person of Christ. Therefore, both are integrally related and form two different expressions, one liturgical and the other pastoral, of the one healing reality.

The charism of healing brings the power of the Spirit, in the name of Jesus Who is the Healer, to bear on the obstacles that are blocking a person from responding to the grace of conversion. It enables spiritual maturity and solid human growth to take place in a particular person. Sometimes it is a simple yet profound work of the goodness and compassion of God's mercy for an individual. Healing itself never stands by itself, but is always in relationship to other aspects of Christian growth and maturity which the charism of healing assists in changing. One of the dangers of encouraging individuals to focus too much on their need for healing is that it can easily embark on a narcissistic or self-absorbed journey in regard to getting healed. Remembering Peter's mother-in-law, we can say that when we receive a spiritual, emotional, or physical healing, it better prepares us to serve others. This gift of healing in the Church brings about zeal for holiness, and to assist individuals to become Missionary Disciples. It is very important for individuals who have been healed and want to serve to learn how to actively share their faith. Healing softens the heart and infuses compassion which enables a person to serve the marginalized with humble and affectionate care. Finally, the wonderful operation of the grace of this gift calls a person higher, to desire to live and lead others to live holier lives.

❀ Chapter Four ❀

Personal Holiness and the Gift of Healing

"Be perfect just as your heavenly Father is perfect" (Matthew 5:48). Personal holiness is the goal for living in the Kingdom of God on earth. The Beatitudes (Matthew 5:3-10) lay out for us the spiritual organizational plan of life in the Kingdom of God under the New Covenant. Then in the next two chapters Matthew proceeds to present the stipulations which are the ideal fulfillment of the Ten Commandments in terms of one's relationship to God and one another. The desired and practical outcome of the charismatic gift of pastoral healing is personal holiness. Excessive focus on spiritual healing while neglecting the essential aspect of Christian human maturity is a mistake. The development of virtues, identified as the powers of the soul aided by grace, which assist in overcoming character weaknesses and promoting moral and human maturity, are absolutely necessary for personal Christian holiness. We need the **Grace of the Renewal** if we are going to fulfill our Catholic identity as potential saints, missionaries, and martyrs. Each individual who has received Christian baptism in water is called to grow into a full blown saint within the community of the Church. The reason for this is that each individual is to fulfill God's plan for His glory and our salvation. When

we cooperate with the Lord's abundant merciful grace by growing in virtue, we gradually step into our identity as a missionary who proclaims and witnesses to the Resurrection of Jesus and the Good News of the Gospel. The good Lord gives each of us the graces we need, and according to the gift of faith we receive the means to participate through our Catholic identity in God's unique design for our personal holiness, and His plan for our life.

What are the consequences of the practice of the "charism of healing" in the pastoral life of the Church? What are some of the benefits, fruits, and rewards derived from receiving the healing that a person may need in one's life? Christians are those who think and live as closely as possible in accordance to God's will. They desire to live guided and nourished by the Holy Spirit, a life worthy of true sons and daughters. And this entails realism and fruitfulness. Those who let themselves be led by the Holy Spirit are realists; they know how to survey and access reality. They are also fruitful; their lives bring new life to birth all around them. Our life's vision is the operative agent that enables us to consciously cooperate with God's plan for our life in all its aspects.[12] Jesus articulated many times in the Gospels that our desire at all times and in all circumstances should be to do the Father's will. This should also be our desire as we gradually mature in the spiritual life. Our life vision then is crucial in accomplishing this task. Our spiritual vision needs structure; "the new wine needs new wineskins."

Under the inspiration of the Holy Spirit, the Church became aware of a beautiful Sacramental way of life. As a community and as individuals we have the daily opportunities of a rich and fruitful encounter with Christ in a personal manner through our sacramental system. The gift of the special charisms found in 1 Corinthians 12:4-11 have been given to us by the

---

12   Pope Benedict XVI, *"A Vision for Life"*, Magnificat, 2016

Lord to enhance and support an abundant life of grace in our individual and communal daily life. This all flows from our Sacramental life and God's enlightenment and action in specific situations. However, a certain caution and humility is necessary in our walk with the Lord in cooperating with these special gifts of grace. Without a well-grounded training and understanding it is easy to misinterpret His will in using these gifts to know God's will. It is not only necessary to know what God's will is, but it is also necessary to know when and how it should be carried out. St. Teresa of Avila wrote that many good and divinely inspired works were destroyed (she used the term "ended on the ash heap") by individuals not giving careful discernment to the when and how, even when the initial inspiration was from the Lord. The vision and desire we have for serving in and renewing the Church may be from the Lord. However, there still remains questions of *"the when and how"* as part of the process when we act on what we believe God wants in particular circumstances and concrete situations. The abundance of grace in carrying out God's will is fruitful when we engage in proper dialogue, discernment, and methods of testing when we are preparing for action.

❦ Chapter Five ❦

Christian Spirituality is Trinitarian

Many attempted and successful reform movements outside the visible structures of the Catholic Church engage in a strong emphasis on the person of Jesus. Sometimes we meet this type of attitude in the statement, "Jesus alone saves"; allowing for the fact that this reality is certainly true, but the temptation there is to forget or infrequently emphasize the roles of the Father and the Holy Spirit. For example, some of these reform movements who consider themselves as churches will singularly proclaim that an individual can be baptized only in the name of Jesus. The Catholic Church baptizes in the name of the Father, the Son, and the Holy Spirit. This is for Catholics a prophetic and doctrinal proclamation of the reality of receiving in Jesus the complete salvation of God the Father, Son, and the Holy Spirit as One. In the words of St. Bonaventure, the source of Sacred Scripture was not human research but divine revelation. This revelation comes "from the Father of Light from whom the whole concept of fatherhood in heaven and on earth derives" (See James 1:17). From Him, through Jesus Christ his Son, the Holy Spirit enters into us. Then, through the Holy Spirit, who allots and apportions His gifts to each person as He wishes, we receive the gift of faith, and through faith Christ lives in our hearts. So we come to know Christ, and this knowledge becomes the main source of a firm understanding of the truth of all sacred Scripture, but also that we might have everlasting life. When we do live that life we shall understand fully, we shall love completely, and our desires will be totally satisfied. Then, with all our needs fulfilled, we shall truly know *"the love that surpasses understanding and so be filled with the fullness of God"* (Ephesians 3:19).

What is the point here? The sovereign truth is that by virtue of Divine Revelation, Christian spirituality is Trinitarian spirituality. This has profound implications for having a personal relationship with God.

In the interior experience of this relationship for a Christian maturing in the grace of a personal relationship with God, it is essential for an individual to be aware of a threefold dynamic interactive balance. Knowledge of this balance results in the understanding and experience of a triad personal relationship with the living God in the person of Jesus Christ. The necessary maturing in this Trinitarian relationship occurs in the practice of a meaningful life of prayer engaging in conversation, communication, and communion with the living God.

Rooted in the Revelation of the Trinity is the call to Christian holiness. All Christians are called to the fullness of the Christian life and the perfection of Christian charity: *"be perfect as your heavenly Father is perfect"* (Mark 5: 48). The Gospel of grace, which is the power of salvation, is a gift of God's love revealed through the person of Jesus. The Gospel of grace is the perfection here on earth of the divine law, natural and revealed. It reveals the mystery of Christ and expresses His work, especially in the Sermon on the Mount. It is also the work of the Holy Spirit, and through Him it becomes the source of charity. *"I will establish a New Covenant with the house of Israel...I will put My laws into their minds, and*

I will write them on their hearts, and I will be their God and they shall be My people" (Jerimiah 31:31, 33). The New Covenant is the grace of the Holy Spirit given to the faithful through faith in Christ. It works through charity; it uses the Beatitudes in order to teach us what is to be done, and makes use of the Sacraments to give us the grace to do it. Grace then is first and foremost the gift of the Spirit who justifies and sanctifies us. All Christians are called to the fullness of the Christian life and the perfection of charity. All are called to holiness.[13]

Given this biblical and evangelical mandate, the following is a brief summary of the spiritual journey that we all make, a path to holiness according to one's vocation in life. When we are baptized through faith in Christ, we receive the active presence and power of divine grace. All our sins are forgiven; however, the negative effects of sin remain and eventually exert themselves in various ways. Sin appears in our life as a principle of narcissistic disorder. It is in this context that our glorified Lord undertakes His saving work in the heart of a person by the action of purgation: purification, illumination, and transforming union. While we by nature are open to God, by a "second nature" we are encased in layers of sinfulness that close us to the dynamism which lies at the very center of our heart. Thus there is need for conversion and purgation. Grace is not successful in us without the Cross: according to St. Bonaventure, the giving up of self and the finding of self in God. The cross is a cruciform structure which stands at the very basis of the life of grace, reflecting the fact that conversion is a constant process in the spiritual journey. And conversion places a cross between the tendency to exist for oneself and the call to exist with and for others.

The second action calls to mind the variety of ways in which spiritual light enters our being, **illumination.** God is the primal light from which beams of light emanate into our

13   New Catechism of Catholic Church, Section III, Life in Christ, #'s 1692 -1698

being. With spiritual light we see with the light of our spirit. The role of the Holy Spirit is to draw us into conformity with Jesus the Word and thus into the relation of the Word to the Father.

The third action is called **perfection or transforming union.** It is also known in terms of its effect, as consummation or union. This is the goal of an individual's spiritual journey. It is the presence of the Spouse that sets the heart aflame with the desire of love. These three actions happen in the soul interchangeably. All three happen in all three dimensions in some way in the spiritual journey; three functions that are involved in different ways of the spiritual journey. The person therefore arrives at an experience of peace in his living knowledge of truth and in his experience of the unitive power of love. "Loving Savior, be pleased to show yourself to us who knock, so that in knowing you we may love only you, love you alone, desire you alone. . . inspire in us the depth of love that is fitting for you to receive as God. So may your love pervade our whole being, possess us completely, and fill all of our senses, that we may not know any other love, but the love for you who are everlasting."[14] In this sense, it enjoys a foretaste of heavenly beatitude. This reality is attained not in isolation but in a living relation with other human beings. We may conclude that the spiritual struggle against the egoistic, possessive, dominating self requires **vigilance, sobriety, and purity of heart.** It also requires a willingness to embrace a life of life-giving repentance as a disciple and ongoing conversion, with the goal of gradually attaining the beatitude of some degree of transforming union.

---

14   *The Spirituality of St. Bonaventure* by Zachary Hayes

Chapter Six

Renewal and Reform:
New Wine and New Wineskins

"People do not pour new wine into old wineskins. If they do, the skins burst, the wine spills out, and the skins are ruined. No, they pour new wine into new wineskins, and in that way both are preserved" (Matthew 9: 17). The Church is only a little over fifty years into the spiritual renewal under the umbrella of Vatican Council II. However, genuine renewal in the Church consists in more than the process of spiritual renewal. It also encompasses reform which includes the structures in a certain manner. There is understandably a strong resistance to changing or developing new structures, but the fact is that some structures will necessarily need to be changed to accommodate the new wine. *"And he replied, every scribe who has been instructed in the kingdom of heaven is like the head of a household who brings from the storeroom both the new and the old"* (Matthew 13: 52).

For evangelical Catholics who are seeking a deeper Christian way of life men's and women's small groups are very helpful. It is important for each local parochial unit or community to develop a plan of preparation for individuals who would like to be a part of a small faith sharing group. A preparation approach for small group work would include simple training in communication, the basics of prayer and praise, and the various elements of spiritual formation, teaching on discipleship, and the importance of Christian service for doing mercy work.

Most of us are challenged by change, and more so as we get older. It is not a matter of discontinuing the solid structures of our parochial entities, but to develop new structures in order to adjust to a more relationship based parish community. In preparing for the future life in the Church, it will be necessary to utilize collaborative and subsidiary styles of leadership, where the focus is more on relationships than on functionality. We need to change some structures and create new ones. A wise steward knows how to take out of the storehouse things both old and new.

In addition to supporting and creating small communities where individuals have experienced mature spiritual renewal centered in the Lordship of Jesus, we also need to have committed persons in small faith sharing, growth, and formation groups that respond to the call of discipleship. These groups would also benefit by opportunities for praise and worship. A series of preparation and training programs that would undertake education and instruction about these possible entities would also be necessary. It may be useful to teach individuals how to exercise the pastoral charism of healing in appropriate situations. Also, it seems necessary to try and expand the gift of the empowerment in the Holy Spirit, which many have experienced in the recent movements in the Church, into broader arenas of church life, like mercy works, and other endeavors. The training of lay leaders on how to pray with others they attempt to serve in the missionary outreaches of evangelization and mercy work is necessary.

It appears that members of the Church in the future will have the opportunities to enjoy small-group personal faith sharing, discipleship training, methods of evangelization, and other missionary activity. Most important is the resurgence of the desire for personal sanctification and holiness in committed members of the Church by making the methods available to achieve these objectives; primarily teaching in meditation and personal prayer, which gradually leads to a life of contemplation in the ministrations of Divine Love. Jesus is breathed into the heart of a person by the divine breath of the Holy Spirit. The role of the Spirit is to draw a person into a greater conformity with Jesus, and thus in relationship with Jesus to the Father. This is the heart of the whole mystery of Christ. The glorified Lord through the Holy Spirit becomes the interior of the soul, and provides the deepest experience of loving union with God, which draws one beyond all that can be imagined or conceived. Obviously these changes take time and come about slowly; wisdom, patience, charity, and the willingness to take some risks is necessary. It seems that the time is now to begin putting the new wine into some well discerned and chosen new wineskins!

✿ Chapter Seven ✿

Relational Evangelization, Disciples, who are Missionaries of Atonement

Over the last number of years in the Church the jargon of evangelization has been rampant in many situations. I have heard leaders attempt to justify what they are doing to serve others as the new evangelization. I would certainly grant that these individuals possess a spirit and wish for evangelization, but the expected results from their endeavors have not materialized. What results should I be looking for? I would look for persons to change and experience Jesus personally and not just know about Him; become alive with a new love for the Gospel, a new awareness of the operation of grace within them, and deeper yearning to grow in the love of God and a desire to share their faith and serve others. In many parochial units in the United States there are programs that attempt to explain and teach others about evangelization.

There is certainly a place in the life of the Church for programmatic evangelization, which can be relationally based. Relational evangelization demands the ability to share one's experience of life-giving repentance, conversion, and growth in faith in the Lord, and be able to witness as to how the Lord has worked personally in one's life. Relational evangelization is personal evangelization. There are two things necessary for relational evangelization; one is a healthy and accurate knowledge of self, and the other is the personal experience of the Lord's work in one's spiritual and human growth. The dynamic of various types of small groups is very useful for the work of evangelization. When individuals receive the healing that they need, they almost automatically respond with a wonderful desire to share the Good News with others.

The three key "mountains" of Revelation in the Word of God are Creation, the Covenant, and the Kingdom of God. We live in the New Creation through our Covenant with God in the Person of Jesus Christ, as we, living in the Church Community, are committed to establishing and building up the Kingdom of God on earth. One of the most important ways in which we accomplish this task is through the unique ministry of evangelization and the power of answered prayer by undertaking the mission of being a **missionary**. This evangelical service of discipleship is possible in all walks of life, and can be practiced by individuals of all ages.

What is the mission of a **missionary Intercessor** who practices intercession, reparation, and atonement? Again the model is going to be Jesus himself. Jesus is our High Priest and King *"who is heir of all things and through whom He created the universe, who is the refulgence of his glory, and the very imprint of His being, and who sustains all things by His mighty word"* (Hebrews 1: 2-3). Because He remains forever, He has a priesthood that does not pass away. Therefore, He is able to save those who approach God through Him, since He lives forever to make intercession for them (see Hebrews 7: 24-25). We ourselves are eternally connected to Jesus in doing intercession, *"Jesus died outside the gate, to sanctify the people by His own blood. Let us go to Him outside the camp, bearing the insult which he bore"* (Hebrews 13:12-13); it is the eternal glorified Lord Jesus, together with His Mystical Body who makes intercession before the throne of the Father for mercy and grace.

Our mission then is to be missionary disciples who by word and example proclaim the Good News as witnesses of the Resurrection, and practice powerful Christ-centered intercession, reparation, and atonement. Frequently we can slip into a surface approach to intercession. Prayers of intercession can be very vague or too general in their design. The results usually seem distant or powerless when the content of the prayer is expressed. This vacuum of powerlessness is usually not very helpful for individuals who want to embrace a meaningful and faith-filled approach to the ministry of intercession, which is very important in the spiritual and material life of the community. Also there is much more to the ministry of intercession than praying with good intention for various types of assistance from the Lord. In becoming more specific we need to understand the notion of reparation. When praying to the Lord when sin is involved, either personally, in group situations, and in the Nation, the necessity of reparation and restitution is highlighted. And more of an integral attention to reparation and atonement is needed. The primacy of Jesus' atoning suffering and death is primarily focused on our redemption, and making amends in Jesus for humankind turning away from the glorious love of the Father, and humankind's tremendous need and desire to repay Love with atoning love. The ministry of intercession involves all three: intercession in times of need for help, reparation for sin, and atonement to a loving and merciful Father in union with the glorified Jesus. Therefore, when one responds to the call to embrace a ministry of intercession, all three become one. And the desire to do the ministry as a missionary involves all three types of intercession becoming one entitled: **missionary of atonement.**

71

In God becoming man in the mystery of the Incarnation, the Word made Flesh suspended the operation of His divine nature. Nevertheless, in His Person He did not lose His divine glorified nature even in the moments on the Cross when He cried out, *"My God, my God why have you forsaken me?"* (Mark 15:34). One person in His divine and human natures, He was the supreme offering of love to the Father. Through His human nature, Jesus sacrificed Himself as a victim of love on the Cross. Now in His glorified state after the Resurrection, He continually draws us to Himself as One Person with two natures. And we, in union with Him as the Mystical Body of Christ, intercede to the Father through intercession, reparation, and atonement. In union with Jesus we are one with Him in the power of the Cross, the Resurrection, and the Holy Spirit when we exercise power centered intercession and atonement, pleading for mercy and grace at the throne of the Father. This ministry we do is in union with Jesus and the Holy Spirit, "In the same way the Spirit comes to the aid of our weakness; for we do not know how to pray as we ought, but the Spirit itself intercedes with inexpressible groanings. And the One who searches hearts knows the intention of the Spirit, because it intercedes for the holy ones according to God's will" (Romans 8:26-27). "Is it Christ Jesus who died, rather was raised who also is at the right hand of God, who indeed intercedes for us?" (Romans 8: 34). The primary emphasis on atonement reveals: AT-ONE-MENT. Dynamic love is the power center of atonement because we are one with Jesus in the Spirit, and living in the atoning love of the Father is the deep-level imitation of Jesus in the Spirit.

Therefore, since we are united with Jesus, we then have the responsibility to do all He did while on earth, and at the same time join with Him in heaven as He continually intercedes for us to the Father. This means we draw on the power of

Jesus, and know that what we pray for is always heard by the Father. The role of the missionary Intercessor is to pray for the salvation of others, practical needs for the building up the Body of Christ, and offer one's life in atonement and reparation for sin, ours and the sin of all those in the world. Through our intercession by word and deed in the daily acts of our life, we give praise to God, and move closer to the fulfillment of the prayer of Jesus to the Father before his death and resurrection, *"So that we may be one just as we are . . . Consecrate them in truth . . . I pray for them so that they all may be one, as you Father are in Me and I in you . . . so that they may be one as we are one"* (John 17: 6-26). In a word, we are missionaries of atonement.

Not all of the faithful have the ability or are called to make their primary focus verbal faith sharing. However, all are called in a faith-filled missionary spirit to be missionary disciples of intercession. The missionary power of intercessory prayer moves us particularly to take up the task of evangelization. Intercessory prayer does not divert us from true contemplation, since authentic contemplation always has a place for others. This attitude becomes a prayer of gratitude to God for others. It is a spiritual gaze born of deep faith which acknowledges what God is doing in the lives of others. At the same time, it is the gratitude which flows from a heart attentive to others.[15] When evangelizers arise from prayer, their hearts are more open; freed of self-absorption, they are desirous of doing good and sharing their lives with others.

Intercession is like a "leaven" in the heart of the Trinity. It is a way of penetrating the Father's heart and discovering new dimensions which can shed light on concrete situations and change them. What our intercession achieves is God's power, the dynamic power of the Father, Son, and Holy Spirit, where His love, faithfulness, and healing is shown ever more

---

15   The Apostolic Letter of Pope Francis, Evangelii Gaudium, The Joy of the Gospel

clearly in the midst of the power or in an individual person's life. When I quiet my mind and open my heart I become a living conduit of the complete presence and action of the Trinity. I then become a conscious channel of the fullness of the Divinity who acts divinely through my whole being to impart God's powerful love, will, and action for the person or group of persons for which I am doing intercession. In a sense this mysterious presence and action of Love becomes a part of my true and authentic self-Identity.

In union with Mary the Mother of Mercy, we truly take on the tremendous power and spirit of the new evangelization. She is the missionary who draws near to us and accompanies us throughout life, opening our hearts to faith by her maternal love. She becomes essentially a part of my personal self-Identity as a missionary Intercessor of atonement. Pope Francis calls Mary "Star of the new Evangelization". In his Apostolic Exhortation he prays to Mary the Mother of the living Gospel that this invitation to a new phase of evangelization will be accepted by the entire ecclesial community.

I would like to try and express some of the key elements which make up being a missionary intercessor. I am assuming that only when a person has experienced a significant amount of the Grace of the Renewal will he/she be in a position to discover an enlightened and rich meaning in being a missionary disciple of atonement. Jesus, of course, is our model. Jesus, the Son of God, is the great High Priest, who before the throne of mercy and grace makes continual intercession for us to the Father. Through our Baptism we are one with Him in the Mystical Body, and as such we are partners of unequal status with Him in his intercession before the Father. Therefore, the categories that comprise the intercessory Priesthood of Jesus apply, in a different degree and dimension, to us as well. Jesus' primary reason of love for the sacrificial offering of His body and the shedding of His blood was to restore to the Father what had been taken away from Him by the sin of humankind, secondarily for our salvation. We have entered into the New Creation through the primacy of Jesus, and serve with Him in the work of the restoration of the Kingdom of God. In union with Him, we continually intercede to the Father until Jesus comes again to finally restore fully the Kingdom of God in heaven and on earth. This mission that we have been called to is very important, and our intercessory union with Jesus in all its practical ramifications fulfills all the features of our sharing more deeply in the Primacy of Love in the person of the glorified Christ, because the Father has decided to listen to our prayers offered in partnership with His Son.

Again, people are healed because of the compassion and personal love God has for them, but they are also healed so they can better serve as disciples and missionaries of the Gospel in the given situations and circumstances of their lives; they are called to live in Compassion Evoking Love Power (CELP). One of the saints of modern times that most epitomizes this reality is Padre Pio. Throughout most of his life he bore the wounds of Jesus Crucified. In addition to his mystical gifts, he constantly experienced the power of the Passion of Jesus and the new life of the Resurrection, the transforming grace to bring healing to others in all situations of life. In a sense he lived and witnessed to a complete experience of the paschal gifts of the glorified Savior. Padre Pio in his life was truly a missionary disciple of God's mercy.

Reflecting on my own life in the grace-filled experience of the Third Order Franciscan tradition, I find meaning in identifying my personal vision in the charisms of the Cross of Jesus (Crucified Mercy), and the experience of abundant divine Mercy flowing from the pierced heart of the Savior and the power of the Resurrection. I view myself as having received these incredible gifts through the prayers of Francis and Clare. Therefore, I stand firmly in the Tradition of being a Servant of the Cross who is a Servant of Crucified Mercy. My witness as a missionary disciple is to witness to the Resurrection of Jesus by the power and gifts of the Spirit, proclaiming and living an evangelical way of life and serving in every way possible the abundant works of mercy; in this way attempting to bring spiritual freedom to others by using these gifts of grace in the opportunities which are given to me.

The ultimate goal of our earthly life is personal holiness within the Community of the Church. Vatican Council II ushered in a concrete awareness that God was doing something new in the Church. To prepare for the onslaught of the twenty first century and our present world situation, the Lord has poured out a new grace of empowerment for the purpose of spiritual renewal and reform in the Church, especially for Catholic family life. The desire and awareness that something needed to happen to bring about a season of refreshment for empowerment by grace was an idea in the hearts and minds of many before the Council began. Under the inspiration of the Holy Spirit this desire was first fulfilled in a concrete articulation of a theological pastoral vision called the Documents of Vatican II. However, as wonderful as these documents are something more was needed to bring about a practical experience of change in the hearts and minds of members of the Church, namely a conversion through life-giving repentance if you will. This unfolding of the Grace of the Renewal in the Church was provided by the Lord as an actual release of a triadic empowerment experienced as one reality: the Paschal empowerment of the Spirit, the Cross, and the Resurrection as one embrace of Divine love. The most important effect of this paschal mystery of Christ is the resurgence of personal sanctification or holiness in the members of the Church.

The central action of the Grace of the Renewal unfolds a three-fold empowerment which gradually leads to a life of prayer through the ministry of Divine Love. Jesus breathes into the heart of the person by the divine breath of the Holy Spirit. The role of the Spirit is to draw the person into a greater conformity with Jesus, and thus into the relationship of Jesus with the Father. This is the heart of the whole mystery of Christ. The glorified Lord through the Holy Spirit becomes the interior teacher of the soul. In other words, we are transformed by Crucified Love, the power of the Cross, life in the Spirit, and a new power and life in the Resurrection, "to know Him and the power of His Resurrection and the sharing of His sufferings" (Philippians 3:10). This singular and deepest experience of loving union with God is found in that form of love that draws one beyond all that can be imagined or hoped for. Grace is not successful in us without the Cross, the Spirit, and the new life of the Resurrection as an experience of the unitive power of love.

In Chapter Five of *Evangelii Gaudium*, the Apostolic Exhortation written by Pope Francis in 2013, he speaks about the necessity of evangelizers being filled with the Holy Spirit. Spirit-filled evangelizers means evangelizers fearlessly open to the working of the Holy Spirit. The Holy Spirit grants the courage to proclaim the newness of the Gospel with boldness in every time and place, even when it meets with opposition. Spirit-filled evangelization is not the same as a set of tasks dutifully carried out despite one's own personal inclinations and wishes. How I long to find the right words to stir up enthusiasm for a new chapter of evangelization full of fervor, joy, generosity, courage, boundless love and attraction! Yet I realize that no words of encouragement will be enough unless the fire of the Holy Spirit burns in our hearts. A spirit-filled evangelization is one guided by the Holy Spirit, for He is the soul of the Church called to proclaim the Gospel.[16]

---

16   The Apostolic Letter of Pope Francis, Evangelii Gaudium, The Joy of the Gospel

The primary reason for evangelization is the love of Jesus which we have received, the experience of salvation which urges us to even greater love of Him. We need to recover the contemplative spirit which helps us to realize that we have been entrusted with a treasure which makes us more human and helps us to lead a new life. Jesus' whole life, His way of dealing with the poor, His actions, integrity, simple daily acts of generosity, and finally His complete self-giving, is precious and reveals the mystery of His divine life. The Gospel offers us friendship with Jesus and love of our brothers and sisters. A true missionary never ceases to be a disciple; he knows that Jesus walks with him, speaks to him, breathes with him, and works with him. He senses Jesus is alive with him in the midst of the missionary enterprise. In the end, what we are seeking is the glory of the Father; we live and act for *the praise and glory of his grace*" (Ephesians 1:6). The ultimate reason and meaning behind all that we do is the glory of the Father which Jesus sought every moment of His life. When we possess a missionary spirit, it is because we realize Jesus told us that *"By this my Father is glorified, that you bear much fruit . . ."* (John 15: 8).[17] Jesus himself is the model of this method of evangelization which brings us to the very heart of His people; arm in arm with others, we are committed to building a new world, which as a result of a personal decision brings us joy and gives meaning to our lives.[18] If we want to advance in the spiritual life, then, we must constantly be missionaries. The work of evangelization enriches the mind and the heart; it opens up spiritual horizons; it makes us more and more sensitive to the workings of the Holy Spirit, and it takes us beyond our limited spiritual constructs. A committed missionary knows the joy of being a spring which spills over and refreshes others.[19]

17   Ibid., No. 266
18   Ibid., No. 268-270
19   Ibid., No. 272

Christ, now raised and glorified, is the wellspring of our hope, and He will not deprive us of the help that we need to carry out the mission which He has entrusted to us. Christ's resurrection is not an event of the past; it contains a vital power which has permeated this world; it is an irresistible force. Each day in our world beauty is born anew. The power of the Resurrection rises anew through the storms of the universal history of creation, and our own personal storms and struggles in life. Such is the power of the Resurrection, and all who evangelize are instruments of its power. Christ's Resurrection everywhere calls forth seeds of the new world of the new creation. The Holy Spirit works as, when and where He wills; we entrust ourselves without expecting to see striking results. We know only that our commitment is necessary. Let us learn to rest in the tenderness of the arms of our Father amid our creative and generous commitment. Let us move forward![20]

---

20   Ibid., No. 278-279

Chapter Eight

Impact of Three Marian Shrines

In 1858 Mary appeared to Bernadette Soubirous near Lourdes in France. She identified herself as the Immaculate Conception and called the people to conversion. Mary asked Bernadette to tell the priests to build a church on that spot. The result of this apparition is the large famous shrine at Lourdes dedicated to physical healing. If one travels to the Shrine, that person will see at the pool at Lourdes many crutches and other implements of the disabled. People usually go there for physical healing; some are physically healed. However, almost everyone who travels there receives emotional and spiritual healing.

There are few people in the world who have the resources or opportunity to go to Lourdes. Realizing this fact, we may miss the real point of the existence of the Shrine, which is: The Shrine is a sacramental sign or symbol of the healing that the Lord wants to happen in all who seek Mary's intercession. Mary witnesses to us a life empowered by the Holy Spirit and the fruitful use of the spiritual gifts, especially for evangelization, merciful service, and the renewing and the building up of the Body of Christ. She is so receptive and willing to act with us and in us. This loving action of Mary leads to wisdom and maturity as we struggle to build faith-filled evangelizing fellowships and communities. These graces change us as we slowly grow in wisdom and maturity, reflecting on God's communication and action in our daily life of prayer. When Mary is actively present she brings people together that enables people to grow as merciful missionary disciples of Jesus.

Not long ago I spent some time in Mexico City, living in a parish about one half hour from the Shrine of Our Lady of Guadalupe. In my first visit I was astounded at how huge the Shrine is, involving four different churches which comprise the Basilica, the name given the shrine by the local gentry. There are thousands daily visiting the Shrine, and on December 12, the feast of Our Lady, it is impossible to drive a car within two or three miles of the Shrine. Pope John Paul II recommended that the Shrine of Our Lady of Guadalupe in La Crosse, Wisconsin be named after her because she is for all of the Americas, both the South and North.

During my second visit, I discovered in the smallest Church the preservation of the little house of Juan Diego. The grace I received was the realization of the necessity of growing in a similar humility in serving the mission God has given the Virgin. Our Lady of Tepeyac, the name of the region and the hill where the apparitions of Mary occurred, appeared to be pregnant and ready to give the new life of her Son to her people. The symbol of her pregnancy conveys abundant life and brings the healing Mercy of her Son to the poor. Putting together both of these gifts of grace from the two Shrines, we are to seek the Lord for genuine growth in holiness and the healing we need through Mary's intercession to live the abundant life of Christ in our life situations. However, this growth and transformation requires from us a cooperation and commitment from each one of us to respond to the grace of God, and the following of the "plan of action" which Mary lays out for us in the majority of her apparitions, which is a life of prayer and on-going conversion as merciful penitents.

Our Lady of Fatima, the third Shrine whose 100th anniversary we celebrated in 2017, calls individuals of the 20th and 21st centuries to put faith in the Virgin Mother who promises the abundant blessings of her Son. The central message of Fatima was proclaimed at the very beginning of a century of world-wide wars, and now the abominable wars of terrorism, which present the real possibility of leading the human race to utter self-destruction. Mary predicted the Second World War and warned against the grave threat of Communism. Her message given to the three children and to the world was a universal action plan: quoting the act of Consecration prayed by Pope John Paul II at Fatima, "We have recourse to your protection, holy Mother of God . . . " "Behold, as we stand before you, Mother of Christ, before your Immaculate Heart, we desire, together with the whole Church, to unite ourselves with the consecration, which for love of us, your Son made of himself to the Father. For their sake, Jesus said, *'I consecrate myself that they also may be consecrated in truth'* (John 17: 19). We wish to unite ourselves with our Redeemer in this his consecration for the world and for the human race, which in His Divine Heart has the power to obtain pardon and to secure reparation and atonement." Fr. Sullivan asks, what did Our Lady call for at Fatima?[21] She calls us to respond by living a life free from all fear and to embrace a call to live a life of prayer, penitence, and conversion,[22] if the otherwise inevitable reality of extinction of large groups of peoples, or of humanity itself, is to be avoided. In all her apparitions, the expected fruit occurs when one embraces a new way of life through conversion, prayer, and penance.

---

21   The Fatima Centennial, by James Sullivan, O.P., Magnificat, May 2017, pp. 165, 175

22   Ibid., Call to live a life of prayer, conversion, and penance

Chapter Nine

Mercy of God in the Mission of the Church

Some time ago I was meeting with a longtime friend. The discussion eventually got around to the topic of holiness. She said to me, I asked the Lord recently, what does it mean to be holy? Of course, I then asked her, what did the Lord tell you? She said, he told me if you want to be holy then give your love away! I agreed with her, and responded that if one wants to be a saint, then give your death away! The full gamut of personal holiness in relationship is to give your love, your life and your death away! This is what Jesus did, and this is what it means to imitate Christ. When we imitate Jesus in this manner, we have arrived at the place where the abundance of divine love in our human personhood becomes **Divine Mercy**. Then we become a partner with the Lord in the dispensation of His divine saving and healing mercy. We become a conduit of a tremendously powerful mission. Our identity becomes one of being **a Servant of Mercy who is a Missionary of Atonement.**

The word Atonement indicates "At-one-ment" to reconcile two parties that were estranged who become one. The root meaning of the word centers on reconciliation and expiation, a re-establishment of God's communion with His people in covenant, His people who have offended Him by sin. It is a work of mercy on the part of God, and on the part of humankind. It is the fulfilling of certain things prescribed by God. The highest spiritual sense of Atonement is found in Isaiah 52, in which the meaning concentrates on expiation. Sin is atoned for with a life, the life of the Suffering Servant of Yahweh, as an offering for guilt.

The preeminence of Christ as the crown of the new creation is to reconcile all things to God through Himself; therefore, the personal deeds of the Crucified One is a sacrifice of love undertaken by a mediator who takes the place of sinners. He suffers for them and effects atonement with a personal God moved by pity for them. The tone is one of reconciliation and vicarious expiation. Christ has become a merciful and faithful High Priest before God to expiate the sins of the people; an action of Divine love which totally impacts and brings about a new state of things, centered in the peaceful reconciled relationship between God and man. In the sacrifice of the Cross, atonement has a major powerful miraculous effect. Thus atonement is effected through the blood of Christ. Humankind is justified by a free merciful choice by the Father, in that the Word became flesh and freely chose atonement in order that humankind would be placed in a new relationship to God, to reconcile all things to God through Himself. Whoever and whatever is in Christ is a new creation. Reconciliation means to reunite, to bring back to friendship after estrangement. Reconciliation is a wonderful gift of Divine Mercy. It is in this reality that atonement and reparation have their tremendous significance. Jesus is Crucified Mercy, and as a victim of love has ransomed us from the fear of death and the power of the devil. He has made satisfaction for sin by His redeeming grace, and therefore, we have merited salvation and are made pure (see Colossians 2: 9-16).

If we are called to be missionaries of atonement, then we should be expected to embrace the life-style of a servant of Mercy living as a modern penitent. Penitents, as servants of Mercy, implore God's mercy on all humankind in the world which is undergoing global desperation. A tidal wave of Mercy is needed in view of the current situation in a world where we have abandoned God or pushed Him to the margins of society. The forgiving and healing Mercy of the Lord is needed in the Church because of the wounds of division, immorality, and secularization. Divine Mercy is God's plan revealed as the sum of the Gospel. It is His creative, redemptive, and sanctifying love poured out upon us as sinners. The role of being a servant of Mercy is a demanding one, expressed through the process of expiation by doing reparation and atonement as servants of Mercy in partnership with Crucified Mercy. The goal of love-filled expiation is directed toward nullifying the effects of our sin and the healing of the wounds of our brokenness. We join with the glorified Jesus in the process of expiation, making satisfaction for our sin by undergoing our own death and resurrection, which is the full course of reparation and atonement.

Together with Jesus as Crucified Mercy, we become victims of love consecrated by obedient suffering into a much closer union with him. We are sanctified through appropriating the gift of saving Mercy, and through atonement joining with Jesus in reparation for sin by becoming a "victim of love." Then in the enlightened understanding of the Spirit we will grow in appreciation of our grace-filled share in the Mystery of Christ as victims of love, and gradually grasp the rich meaning of atonement; living At-One-Ment in union with the Father, Son, and Holy Spirit. The experiential graces of this mission of being Servants and Missionaries of Atonement builds on the basic principle of dying and rising as the core of Christian life, and invites us to a level of actualizing graces flowing from special gifts of the Spirit, and the unique and singular charisms of our individual communities and associations in the Church. The Merciful Heart of Jesus becomes the focus and center of this gift of Divine Mercy to the world. As penitent Servants who are Missionaries of Mercy, we put mercy into action. Transformed into His beating Heart of Love, we will receive power to embrace the mission of mercy the Lord asks of us. In the words of the Lord to Sister Faustina, "Speak to the world about my mercy; let all humankind recognize my unfathomable mercy. It is a sign for the end times; after it will come a day of justice. While there is still time let them have recourse to the font of my mercy . . ."[23]

Atonement emphasizes the unifying aspect of reparation, and expiation is geared toward the action of repairing. One points up the work, the other the fruit of unity. Some are called to a special vocation in redemptive suffering love as victims of love. To embrace atonement is living a way of life, as a servant of Mercy. This reality calls for an acceptance to become one with the sufferings of Jesus, and giving our **yes** to God to offering our sufferings in union with the Glorified and Eucharistic Lord as a plea for mercy on each one of us and on the whole world. Christ sanctified suffering to be salvific by his love. **Reparation and Atonement is the disciple's way of life!** Christ invites us to share in his suffering to sanctify and bring salvation to others. Suffering leads to glory! "Suffering is a great grace, through suffering the soul becomes like the Savior; in suffering, love becomes crystallized, the greater the suffering, the purer the love."[24] By the power and fruit of the Passion of Jesus the work of reparation and atonement should be accompanied by a heart of compassion; this increases its fruitfulness, and leads us to the practice of spiritual immolation, which is a necessary consequence.

---

23   *Diary of Sister Faustina*, No. 84
24   Ibid., No. 57

The call to become a Missionary of Atonement is a specific call which does not occur in the abstract. The Son reveals the Father to us through His human nature, His words and actions. Jesus reveals the Father and becomes visible especially in his Mercy. Jesus is Incarnate Mercy; he is Divine Mercy itself. The messianic mission of Jesus is Mercy; therefore, the core and heart of Jesus' life, words and actions is mercy. Jesus is Divine love in the "human condition" and revealed in Scripture, especially through his death on the cross and resurrection. Jesus revealed Divine love as Mercy, which signifies a special power of love. God abounds in steadfast love and mercy through forgiveness. And mercy manifests its true nature when it brings healing, consolation, and restores our dignity and the dignity of the other as a person.

Mercy is the content of the saving work of Christ and it constitutes the power of his messianic mission. But Jesus expected that people's lives should be guided by love and mercy. When the Lord finds life-giving love, repentance, and true forgiveness, he draws people back to grace through love and mercy. Mercy is the content of intimacy with the Lord. Our whole lives express gratitude to Him for His mercy, and as Church we participate in the messianic mission of Jesus by putting mercy into practice, for it equals a love for our neighbor, love as a unifying and elevating power and not only a spiritual transformation.

The full gift of Mercy is revealed in the gracious Atonement of the total self-giving love of Jesus to His Father for all human beings, created in His image and chosen from the beginning to satisfy the fidelity of the Creator and Father in this Son, for grace and glory. The events of the Passion, Death, and Resurrection introduce a radical and fundamental change into the whole course of the revelation of love and mercy in the messianic mission of Christ: "through his stripes we are healed" (Isaiah: 53: 5). This redemption is the ultimate and definitive revelation of the holiness of God, and springs completely from love. It is the love of the Father and the Son, and it completely bears fruit in love which gives humankind access to the fullness of life and holiness that comes from God and involves the revelation of mercy in its fullness. The power of the Cross gives to all the new and definitive grace of the Covenant, which is given to all through the Crucified One, the saving gift of Divine Mercy. It is important to know that believing in the power of the Crucified One means experiencing the life and love of the Father, and believing in this love means believing in mercy. **Atonement is the exercise of the love and power of Divine mercy.** In the temporal phase of human existence, love must be revealed and actualized as mercy. Christ's messianic program of mercy becomes the program of His people, the program of the Church, and the very life of the Church is always centered in the power of the Cross. The inscrutable unity of the Father, Son, and Holy Spirit, in which love contains justice and sets in motion mercy which in turn reveals the perfection of justice.

The power of the Crucified One as a Servant of Mercy cannot be separated from the power of the Resurrection. In his Resurrection, Christ has revealed the God of merciful love, precisely because He accepted the Cross as the way to the Resurrection. And it is for this reason that when we recall the Cross of Christ, His passion and death, the power of our faith and hope are centered on the Risen One, on that Christ who on the evening of the day of the Resurrection stood among them and said, "peace be with you," breathed on them and said to them, "receive the Holy Spirit." Through the powerful anointing and bestowal of the Holy Spirit, He gave His disciples the power to forgive sin, which is the central condition of all forms of healing and the celebration of the Sacraments. Here the Son of God in His Resurrection gave the experience of the power and life of the Resurrection to

His disciples. The giving of this power was not the power of Pentecost, which would come later, but the inexhaustible source of Resurrection power, which is His gift of Divine Mercy (see John 20:23). Let us take a closer look at this passage, which relates to the bestowal of the reconciling power of the gift of the Resurrection of Jesus.

> *"On the evening of the first day of the week, when the doors were locked, where the disciples were, for fear of the Jews, Jesus came stood in their midst and said to them,* **"Peace be with you."** *When he had said this he showed them his hands and his side. The disciples rejoiced when they saw the Lord. Jesus said to them again,* **'Peace be with you. As the Father sent me, so I send you."** *And when he said this, he breathed on them and said to them,* **"Receive the Holy Spirit. Whose sins you forgive are forgiven them, and whose sins you retain are retained"**
>
> — John 20:19-23

On Easter Sunday night in the Upper Room, Jesus had ascended to the Father, and the glorified Lord had the power with the Father to give the Spirit to the disciples. Just what exactly did Jesus confer on the disciples? The glorified risen Lord Jesus on Easter Sunday night appeared as the Divine Son of God in the midst of them, saying, "Peace be with you!"

He immediately revealed **the great mystery of the new creation - universal reconciliation.** He who was raised from the dead by the Father showed them the wounds in His hands and side. He revealed the source of all His power - His glorified wounds and the power of His risen life, the gift of eternal reconciliation. And He gave all his power and life to His disciples, saying again, "Peace be with you." Then he breathed the Spirit on them, and said "The sins you forgive are forgiven them, and who sins you retain are retained."

Peace or Shalom, in the liturgy and in the transcendent message of the Scriptures, means more than a state of mind, of being, or of affairs. It seems to encapsulate a reality and hope of wholeness for the individual within societal relations. This would pertain to the Body of Christ, the Mystical Body, and for the whole world. To say joy and peace, meaning a state of affairs where there is no dispute or war, does not begin to describe the sense of the term. Completeness seems to be at the center of Shalom. When used as a verb it provides a deeper understanding of this term in theology, liturgy, and doctrine - it points to completeness, and it describes actions that lead to a state of wholeness. It describes a process, an activity, a movement towards fullness, atonement. The use of Shalom in the Scriptures always points toward that transcendent action of wholeness. The wholeness of Shalom, through justice and truth, inspires the words of hope for the work expected by the Messiah, and to refer to its revelation (Resurrection of Jesus) as the time of peace, grace of blessing, goodness and grace, and atonement. Shalom can mean completeness, safety, and welfare; and it can also mean to be safe, secure, forgiven, and emphasizes **complete atonement.** It proposes a personal commitment to the reality, action, and transcendence of peace, and obedience, submission, and surrender to God. Shalom is the action of peace bestowed on those living in the NEW CREATION through the action of Atonement.

Therefore, the Grace of the Renewal involves the experience of the three-fold power of the Holy Spirit, the Cross, and the Resurrection, operationally as one power to bring life-giving repentance, conversion, healing, and atonement to every believing person. A missionary of Atonement is one who incorporates intercession, reparation, and atonement as a Servant of Divine Mercy to bring liberation to all who have accepted faith in the Person of Jesus, and is a servant of the fullness of the saving and liberating mercy of the Father, Son, and the Holy Spirit.

All the outpouring of the graces of Divine Mercy, and our ability to respond to these gifts of love as servants of Mercy who are disciples and missionaries of Atonement, come through Mary the mother of Jesus, the mother of Mercy, the mother of the Church. Mary obtained mercy in a particular and exceptional way, as no other person has.[25] She has shared uniquely in the revelation of Mercy. She is the one who has the deepest knowledge of the mystery of God's mercy. She knows its price and how great it is. Her soul was prepared to perceive that mercy which all people share according to the eternal design of the most Holy Trinity. The heart of the mother of the Crucified and Risen One, as the one who has obtained mercy in an exceptional way, in an equally exceptional way merits that mercy through her earthly life hidden in the messianic mission of her Son, was called in a special way to be the mother of that Merciful Love, which Jesus had come to reveal to all, especially the poor, and most especially to those chosen and called to be Missionaries of Atonement. It is together with her and united with her manifold intercession that we become powerful and fruitful missionaries of intercession, reparation, and atonement.

The primary focus of atonement is to make amends and repair for the disregard, dishonor, hatred, and indifference we have shown to the God of love. Our response to this is in union with Jesus' sacrificial offering of love; thus atonement is the unique gift of mercy. The Church must profess and

---

25   *Dives Misericordia, The Encyclical of Divine Mercy* by St. John Paul II, No. 14-15

proclaim God's mercy in all its truth, as it has been handed down to us by revelation. In the daily life of the Church, the truth about the mercy of God is shown by various expressions of personal, communal, and liturgical piety. The realm of daily life is where we encounter the mercy of God and mercy towards others in close harmony with our encounters of the living God, particularly closely and often. *"He who has seen me has seen the Father"* (John 14: 9). The Church lives by this in Her wide experience of faith and also in Her teaching, constantly contemplating Christ, concentrating on Him, His life, Gospel, Cross and Resurrection, on **his whole Mystery,** drawing close to Him in the Mystery of His Heart which enables us to live in the merciful love of the Father, a revelation constituting the atoning mission of the Son of Man.

The Church sees mercy as momentary interior and exterior acts, but also as a permanent attitude, as a state of mind, and a conscious committed lifestyle. The Church seeks to put mercy into practice. Conversion to God always consists in discovering his mercy. Members of the Church are called to give testimony of life, witnessing to the death and resurrection of Jesus. Jesus Christ taught that each one of us not only receives and experiences the mercy of God, but each one of us is called to practice mercy toward others, which leads to conversion and a reform of life. Each one of us attains to the merciful love of God to the extent that we are interiorly transformed in the spirit of love for our brothers and sisters. This authentically evangelical process is not just a spiritual transformation realized anew for all, the empowerment of the Holy Spirit, but it is a whole lifestyle, an essential and continual characteristic of the Christian vocation. It consists in the constant discovery and persevering practice of love as a unifying and elevating power despite all difficulties. In other words, **it is a necessary call and response to become a modern penitent, a missionary disciple of atonement.**

On this basis, being one with the Crucified One, we must also continually purify our own actions and all our intentions in which mercy is understood and practiced as a good done to others. An act of merciful love is only really such when we are deeply convinced at the moment when we perform it, that we are at the same time receiving mercy from the people who are accepting it from us.[26] This principle of mutual mercy is also why we receive an interior cleansing when we practice being a missionary of atonement. If this is not so in us, then we still need more healing and conversion, nor are we yet sharing fully in the magnificent source of merciful love that has been revealed to us by Him.

Let us be mindful of the true relationship between mercy and justice. There is a necessary link between mercy and justice. Justice becomes functional or egoistic philanthropy when caring for the poor is not enriched by the experience of the graces of mercy. This reality is most evident in the whole biblical tradition, and above all by the witness of the messianic mission of the atonement of Jesus Christ. The person who gives becomes more generous when he feels at the same time benefited by the person accepting his gift and visa-versa. The practice of true justice necessitates being engulfed in mercy; the dignity and equality of both parties is preserved in their relationship.

The characteristics of this relationship of mercy, in regard to justice, the essence of the Gospel mandate in the practice of mercy in the parables of the Good Samaritan and the Sheep and Goats, the Judgment of the Nations, are indispensable between those who are closest to one another and rooted in the grace of forgiveness. Mercy becomes the school of daily living when forgiveness is experienced as freedom and when the essential value and dignity of persons is maintained by merciful love.

---

26   Dives Misericordia, No. 14

In *Misericordiae Vultus*, the Extraordinary Jubilee of Mercy, Pope Francis begins by stating that "Jesus Christ is the face of the Father's mercy."[27] These words might well sum up the Christian faith. Mercy has become living and visible in Jesus of Nazareth, reaching its culmination in him, the ultimate and supreme act by which God comes to meet us. Mercy is the fundamental law that dwells in the heart of every person who looks sincerely into the eyes of his brother and sisters on the path of life. Mercy is the bridge that connects God and man, opening our hearts to the hope of being loved forever despite our sinfulness. Because at times we are called to gaze even more attentively on mercy so that we may become a more effective sign of the Father's action in our lives. This is why I proclaimed an Extraordinary Jubilee of Mercy as a special time for the Church, a time when the witness of believers might grow stronger and more effective. On the day I open the Holy Door, it will become a Door of Mercy through which anyone who enters will experience the love of God who consoles, pardons, and instills hope. This Holy Year is to be an extraordinary one of **grace and spiritual renewal,** the Gospel must be proclaimed in a new way. During this year we entrust the life of the Church, all humanity, and the entire cosmos to the Lordship of Christ, **asking him to pour out his mercy upon us like the morning dew, so that everyone may work together to build a brighter future.**[28]

Mercy is the foundation of the Church's life. The time has come for the Church to take up the joyful call to mercy once more. It is time to return to the basics and bear the weaknesses and struggles of our brothers and sisters. Mercy is the force that reawakens us to new life and instills in us the courage to look to the future with hope. In a word, wherever there are Christians, everyone should find an oasis of mercy. In silence,

27   Misericordiae Vultus, The Extraordinary Jubilee of Mercy, Introduction, Pope Francis, 2016
28   Ibid., No.15

contemplate God's mercy and develop it as a lifestyle. Now in this season of mercy each one of us should enter a time of prayer, penance, and sacrifice, this is a sign that mercy is also a goal to reach and requires dedication and sacrifice. This lifestyle leads to conversion, where we will find the strength to embrace God's mercy and dedicate ourselves to being merciful with others as the Father has been with us.

This season of mercy is the context for understanding what it means to be a penitent. The true pilgrim becomes a modern penitent. Penitents are servants of mercy who are disciples of the Crucified One who live the lifestyle of being Missionaries of Atonement. In the practice of this penitential way of life, we give our whole self to the love of God, victims of love for Him who has been so dishonored. Servants of Mercy are Missionaries of Atonement who give back "love for Love." Penitents become healers of the wounded in society and those who are broken-hearted. The Church will be called even more to heal these wounds, to assuage them with the oil of consolation, to bind then with mercy and cure them with solidarity and vigilant care. Let us not fall into humiliating indifference or a monotonous routine that prevents us from discovering what is new! Let us ward off destructive cynicism! Let us open our eyes and see the misery of the world, the wounds of our brothers and sisters who are denied their dignity, and let us recognize that we are compelled to heed their cry for help! May we reach out to them and support them so that they can feel the warmth of our presence, our friendship, and our fraternity! May their cry become our own, and together may we break down the barriers of indifference that too often reign supreme and mask our hypocrisy and egoism!

Pope Francis highlights that the Christian people should reflect on the **corporal and spiritual works of mercy.** It will be a way to reawaken our conscience, too often grown dull in the face of poverty. And let us enter more deeply into the

heart of the Gospel where the poor have a special experience
of God's mercy. Jesus introduces us to these works of mercy in
His preaching and action so that we can know whether or not
we are living as His disciples. Let us rediscover these corporal
and spiritual works of mercy. Mercy will bring to the fore the
richness of Jesus' mission, and bring love and healing in the
power of the Gospel through the full **Grace of the Renewal.**
Christians are called to witness by their faith and love these
actions of mercy and evangelization. As Servants of Mercy in
the spirit of being Missionaries of Atonement, may we pray!

*Oh Eucharistic and merciful Sacred Heart of
Jesus, in the power of Your Passion and in the
love of the Cross, I love You and trust You, for
You have atoned for my sins, our sins, and the
sins of the whole world. Through Your pierced
heart, blood and water poured forth as a fount
of mercy for us. I love You and trust You. Eternal
Father, I offer You The Body, the Blood, the
Soul and Divinity of Your dearly beloved Son,
Our Lord Jesus Christ, in atonement for our
sins and the sins of the whole world.*

ᐸᔑ Chapter Ten ᔐᐳ

Evangelization: Prayer, Preparation, and Faith Sharing

Three considerations should be given for an over-all perspective on evangelization:

1. The goals of evangelization.
2. Prayer, counsel, and teaching to prepare individuals to be mature missionary disciples who can do relational evangelization.
3. The training and formation to develop a life of prayer and holiness.

When some decide to serve in the Church by personal evangelization, they usually come to the realization that they do not know how to do evangelization or personally share their faith. This is not just a few people, but is actually where most individuals are when they want to share their personal faith. Some authors in their talks and writings point out that there are a number of basic reasons why Catholics avoid faith sharing or doing evangelization. Some are unaware of who they are as persons. Many internally can experience various fears, self- consciousness, or other anxiety issues. In this day and age many are ignorant of the Catholic faith, and some are just self-absorbed or lazy. Therefore, in order for persons to grow into a mature ability to evangelize or share their personal faith, they need to receive some degree of healing and also faith formation. Any group or association would need to provide practical methods and training on how to do evangelization, and some sort of small group opportunities. It is a broken world in which we live. Many dedicated individuals are carrying wounds from their heritage, personal hurts, and the negative spirit of the world which has affected their thinking, feelings, and behavior. It would surprise me if one could find any individual who doesn't need some degree of personal spiritual renewal or some degree of personal prayer.

In the first part of this document, I reviewed some key individuals in the Catholic Church and several Protestant contributors who have specialized in the ministry of inner healing. Each one specializes in a unique dimension. However, the basic model for each one is the same. It is the person of Jesus and what He said and did in the Scriptures. Yet in Scripture, Jesus doesn't engage in a detailed description of a systematic approach one does in a specific healing session, He just meets people where they are in their need and does the ministry. Each minister I reviewed worked faithfully in order to develop a specific and effective approach, and highlights a key feature in their ministry. In addition to that, it is of primary importance in a given ministry session to discern where an individual is in regard to his needs, and what approach would be most effective in removing the obstacles that would get in the way of a sincere individual who desires to serve the Lord.

☘ Chapter Eleven ☘

The Grace of the Renewal:
In the Spirit, through the Power of the Cross, and
by the Glory of the Resurrection

The spiritual experience of the **Grace of the Renewal** in
the Church is a threefold reality of one empowerment, which
is fully lived out in a deepening of our unique relationship
with God, the dynamic life in the Father, Son, and Holy
Spirit within the Church community. It may be experienced
by several intense highlights of grace; nevertheless, it occurs
as a process of transformation and formation. It is necessary
to offer a well-planned preparation to assist individuals to
receive initially the release of the power of the Holy Spirit,
as an actualizing grace of personal empowerment together
with the appropriate charisms. This should naturally and
supernaturally lead to an experience and knowledge of an
empowerment of the Cross of the Crucified One, and the
subsequent graces of living a new life in the power and glory
of the Resurrection, in this time of the New Creation. This
experience may happen by multiple offerings of personal and
evangelical formation. When one just focuses on the first part
only, the release of the power of the Holy Spirit, the enthusiasm

of the initial experience tends to die out as we continue an excessively busy life, which can easily over take the experience of the empowerment of the Spirit.

The question then arises as to just what should be reasonably expected in an individual who commits to a maturing growth in the Church's **Grace of the Renewal**? And how do we structure opportunities to meet the necessary features of that person's gradual transformation and growth? What are the basic considerations and features of this journey? The first reflection that could be addressed is: what does it mean to mature and grow in the **Grace of the Renewal**? Those have gone through a well-prepared seminar which describes the **Grace of the Renewal** as a release of the power of the Holy Spirit, an emergence in the salvific love and power of the Cross, and a profound experience of power and new life of the Resurrection, should experience growth in personal prayer, freedom from obstacles, begin to meet with others and share the good things of the Lord. At this point each person would be presented with a tool kit, the content of which would be most useful in developing a solid Christian life of love and service. A Christian life embraces a commitment to discover or rediscover the wonderful graces of generosity and personal holiness which are present in the gifts at work in the lives of others. Some of the things contained in the tool kit would be; learning the ways and means of growing in a deep life of faith; the importance of daily prayer time, reading the Word of God and meaningful celebrations of the Sacraments. It would establish means to a flexible and tailored personal growth plan, participating in small groups dedicated to the mission of evangelization, learning to pray with others for their particular needs, and helping to develop the living reality of Pentecost in the lives of others.

Pope John Paul II said: "I hope that the spirituality of Pentecost will spread in the Church as a renewed incentive to prayer, holiness, communion and proclamation." The outpouring of the Spirit, sent by the Father and the glorified Christ upon those gathered in the Upper Room was the anointing that empowered the early Church of the New Creation. We are to live our daily lives in the grace of this anointing. We are not meant to live the teachings of Jesus simply by our own efforts and will power, but through the empowering of the Holy Spirit that enables us to share in Jesus' anointing that He received in the River Jordan and by the power of His death and Resurrection.[29]

It is necessary to live a life in the Spirit to invite individuals to live a life-style in the fullness of the Holy Spirit as a total grace of the Church's Spiritual Renewal. Keeping in mind that one the goals of the Church's Grace of Renewal is to form small discipleship groups of Missionary Disciples of Atonement. How can we develop a renewal seminar or a tiered program, which blends the release of the power of the Spirit, wisdom, glory, and the power of the Cross, and the power of the new life of the Resurrection in an experiential process of transformation? This transformation process has the goal of personal sanctification and formation of Missionary Disciples and Servants of Mercy, imbued with an evangelical focus, a devoted missionary spirit, a solid desire to experience faith-filled communal relationships as brothers and sisters, and devotion to the Lord God, which feed the thirsting soul for an intimate union of love. This challenging approach could augment and enhance the experience and present the complete empowerment of the renewal gift of the Paschal Mystery as both a personal and communal experience.

---

29   Celebrating a Charismatic Jubilee by Fr. Bob Hogan, BBD, p.18

Chapter Twelve

Models of the Church

"Write down the vision clearly upon the tablet, so that one can read it readily. For the vision still has its time, presses on to fulfillment, and will not disappoint; if it delays, wait for it, it will surely come, it will not be late" (Habakkuk 2: 2-3). In any work or enterprise which a group undertakes, it is very important for the group to have a clear **vision** of what they are about. This is especially true of the Church. The biblical understanding of having a vision for a specific spiritual or theological entity rooted in reality requires an understanding which is not just an idealistic concept but also determines an application in and implication for reality. All individuals, groups, and ecclesial bodies need to have a **vision** for their exercise and action in achieving the goals of their operation.

I would like to point out that the notion of discipleship is best considered within the context of reviewing the nature of the Church and its mission and ministry. In 1992, Cardinal Avery Dulles wrote a book titled *The Models of the Church*, which attempted to alleviate some of the confusion after the Council as to the nature of the Church coping with the reality of change. His work may also provide a good context to review the notion of Christian discipleship. He identified five basic models and a sub-model, which suggest that the Church could be viewed secondarily as a "Community of Disciples."[30]

1) Institutional model

The first model is the Institutional model. The institutional view defines the Church in terms of its visible structures, especially the rights and powers of its offices. Thus the authority of leadership is vested in clerics and church officers. The priesthood is a divinely ordained channel of divine grace. The strength of the institutional model is in its public, visible manifestation of solidarity. It presents a tangible communion of faith. Unlike the other models, all tests of membership are visible and demonstrable. The weaknesses of the model, however, are also significant. Without other influences, the hierarchy may become rigid and conformist; it could be tempted to substitute the official Church for God, which would be a form of idolatry. Or it could lose its vitality and internal strength by operating on unchanging external images or configurations of the past. Dulles goes on to explain that this is the only model that must not be paramount. He writes, "One of the five models, I believe, cannot properly be taken as primary — and this is the institutional model. Of their very nature, I believe, institutions are subordinate to persons, structures are subordinate to life."[31]

2) Church as Sacrament

This model tends to blend the Institutional model and the Mystical Communion model because of the connecting notion of the life of grace, retaining structure while also promoting a dynamic spiritual life. The structure of human life is symbolic. "The body with all its movements and gestures becomes the expression of the human spirit; the spirit comes

30   The Models of the Church, by Cardinal Avery Dulles, S.J., published in 1992
31   Ibid., p. 189

to be what it is in and through the body." Accordingly, the Church as sacrament is a sign and transmitter of God's grace in the world and through its members. As an embodiment of the grace it signifies, the Church exists as the visible presence of God to the nations. Another important element of this model highlights and affirms that, in the Christian tradition, sacraments are never merely individual transactions. Nobody baptizes, absolves, or anoints himself, and it is anomalous for the Eucharist to be celebrated in solitude. Here again the order of grace corresponds to the order of nature. Man comes into the world as a member of a family, a race, a people.

He comes to maturity through encounter with his brothers and sisters. Sacraments therefore have a dialogic structure. They take place in a mutual interaction that permits the people together to achieve a spiritual breakthrough that they could not achieve in isolation. A sacrament therefore is a socially constituted or communal symbol of the presence of grace coming to fulfillment. The strength of this model is that the church truly is a sign and instrument of grace to its members and the world, while holding in tension the outer (organizational/institutional) and inner (mystical communion) aspects of the Church. Its weakness is that it has little warrant in Scripture and in the early tradition of the Church, and it could lead to a sterile aestheticism and to an almost narcissistic self-contemplation.[32] The sacramental model integrates and blends the other four models.[33] The Sacramental model has found relatively little acceptance among some Protestant churches.

---

32   The summary of Cardinal Dulles' work was composed by Chris Castaldo
33   The integration of the models, composed by Chris Castaldo

3) Church as Mystical Communion

This model demonstrates that the church consists of faithful men and women who are bound together by their participation in God's Spirit through the living glorified Christ. The nature of this unity is not just institutional but also is Spirit-filled, communal, and personal. The goal of the Church in this model is a spiritual or supernatural one. It aims to lead men into communion with the divine. The Church from this point of view is not in the first instance an institution or a visibly organized society. Rather it is a communion of men and women, primarily interior but also expressed by external bonds of creed, worship, and ecclesiastical fellowship. The bond of unity in this model consists of the gifts of the Holy Spirit, though the external bonds are recognized as important in a subsidiary way. The strength of the Church as Mystical Communion is its emphasis on the dynamic community generated by the Holy Spirit in relationship with God and a relationship with brothers and sisters. The potential downside of this model is the danger of it degenerating into mere Christian fellowship without objective theological content. In other words, the communion may exalt and divinize the Church beyond its due. It may also fail to give Christians a clear sense of their identity and mission.

4) The Church as Herald or Proclamation

The herald model differs from the preceding because it makes the 'word' primary and the 'sacrament' secondary. It sees the Church as gathered and formed by the Word of God. The mission of the Church is to proclaim that which it has heard, believed, and commissioned to proclaim. This model is "kerygmatic", for it looks upon the church as a herald — one who receives an official message with a commission to pass it on. Kerygma is the essential core of the Gospel. It invites individuals to experience who Jesus is and what He has done for us. It promotes the power center of the message of Salvation. At the center of this perspective is the proclaiming church, the activity of calling its members to renewal and reformation. The strength of this model is its emphasis on the message of the Gospel and the pursuit of the Great Commission. It can be limited, however, in that it is often devoid of mercy work and service, and can overemphasize the spiritual. This is especially obvious when it focuses too exclusively on witness to the neglect of personal or social responsibility.

5) Church as Servant

The Servant model asserts that the Church should consider itself as part of the total human family, sharing the same concerns as the rest of men. Following in the footsteps of Jesus our Lord, the Suffering Servant, the Church announces the coming of the Kingdom not only in word, through preaching and proclamation, but more particularly in work, in her ministry of reconciliation, binding up wounds, or suffering service, of healing, and works of mercy. In explaining the meaning of the Church as Servant, Cardinal Dulles points out that the term "servant" contains certain ambiguities. It connotes three things: work done not freely but under orders; work to the good of others rather than to the workers' own advantage; and work that is humble and servile. However, in the Gospels the humble and meek servants are not slaves but friends. Living in the vision of the Kingdom of God, we discover, *"whoever remains in me and I in him will bear much fruit, because without me you can do nothing . . . No one has greater love than this, to lay down one's life for one's friends. You are my friends if you do what I command you. I no longer call you slaves, because a slave does not know what his master is doing. I have called you friends; because I have told you everything I have heard from my Father"* (John 15: 5-15). The weakness of the Servant model is observed in the work of those who make good human endeavors and active service in the world more important than spiritual transformation. These proponents would tend to challenge us to believe that the role of the Church in the world is more important than living a dynamic life of evangelical faith and love in and through the person of Jesus Christ.

Integration of the Models

Each one of the models offers insight and positive contributions to our understanding of the Church. When the most genuine and authentic qualities are preserved from each model and integrated together, we realize a stronger ecclesial vision. Each of them brings out certain important and necessary points:

1) The institutional model makes it clear that the Church must be a structured community, and that it must remain the kind of community Christ instituted. Such a community would have to include a pastoral office equipped with authority over the worship of the community, and to represent the community in an official way.

2) The sacramental model brings home the idea that the Church must in its visible aspects—especially in its community prayer and worship—be a sign of the continuing vitality of the grace and place of personal encounter with Christ and of hope for the redemption that He promises.

3) The mystical community model makes it evident that the Church must be united to God by grace and that in the strength of that grace its members must be lovingly united to one another.

4) The kerygmatic model accentuates the necessity of the Church to continue to herald and proclaim the Gospel and to move men to put their faith in Jesus as Lord and Savior.

5) The diaconal or servant model points up the urgency of making the Church contribute to the transformation of the secular life of man, and of impregnating human society as a whole with the values of the Kingdom of God.

Cardinal Dulles recommends the sacramental model because of its ease in integrating all the best elements of the other four models. For blending the values in the various models, the sacramental type of ecclesiology in my opinion has special merit. It preserves the value of the institutional elements because the official structures of the Church give it clear and visible outlines, so that it can be a vivid sign. It preserves the grace-filled mystical model of community, for if the Church were not a communion of love it could not be an authentic sign of Christ. It preserves the dimension of proclamation, because only a reliance on Christ and by bearing witness to Him, whether the message is welcomed or rejected, can the Church effectively point to Christ as the bearer of God's redemptive grace. The Servant model, finally preserves the dimension of worldly service, because without this the Church would not be a sign of Christ the servant. A balance in the models challenges evangelical Catholics to comprise the qualities of mystical tangibility, grace-filled relationships in community, sacramental encounters with the risen and glorified Christ, the experience of proclaiming and witnessing to Jesus as Lord and Savior, and together with the Father, the source of the Spirit and spiritual gifts, kerygma and diaconal servanthood to keep the reality of the message of the Kingdom of God embodied and proclaimed at the cutting edge of life.[34]

A decade or so before the opening of Vatican Council II, the Church was embroiled in an ongoing debate about the nature of the Church. The institutional and sacramental models exclusively constituted the formation and preparation we

---

34   Chris Castaldo ends his article by identifying the key strengths of each model

received for the priesthood back when I entered religious life in 1958. Even to this day, many of the parishes I have visited have continued to emphasize the institutional and sacramental models, with very little attention being given to the other three models. Generally, this is the environment in which I was born, lived my early adult life, and experienced for most of my priesthood. Over these years and by the influence of the Council, the other three models are emerging and struggling to experience a reasonable acceptance and integration. The key is a dynamic growth and balance with a humble openness to move in a positive direction in which the Spirit is leading the Church. At this point it seems the Church needs to discern and embrace a major vector change, following the grace and guidance of the Holy Spirit and good pastoral leadership.

The Models of the Church or its flexible adaption can be a useful tool for discerning the type of spiritual programs, formation offerings, and pastoral services which one would choose for the well-being and growth of the Church community. The vision the models present could make a big difference in the preparation and emphasis one does in preaching and teaching in the community. An appreciation of the models could make a big difference in how we go about presenting discipleship training. The mystical communion, proclamation, and servant models are essential for training people to do evangelization and various types of mercy ministries. Some combination of these three models would be useful in training individuals to pray for others, and make some adjustments in ministering the Sacraments. Knowledge of them would be helpful in relating to other Christians in ecumenical events. It is with an integrated and flexible vision for the appropriate adjustments necessary for a better understanding in the nature of the Church and its dynamic vector changes, in which the following reflections on discipleship are presented.

ᏉChapter ThirteenᏉ

The Call to Christian Discipleship

"On one occasion when a great crowd was following Jesus, he turned to them and said, **'If anyone comes to me without hating his father and mother, his wife and his children, his brothers and sisters, indeed his very self, he cannot be my disciple. Anyone who does not take up his cross and follow me cannot be my disciple . . . In the same way none of you can be my disciple if he does not renounce all his possessions.'** *"*

— Luke 14: 25-33

The key configurations listed in Scripture of being a disciple of Jesus are: the hating of father and mother etc., taking up one's cross, renouncing self, giving up all one's possessions. This teaching of Jesus demands a total and monumental giving of everything. The biblical principles of discipleship

113

articulated by Jesus in the Gospels are essential for every baptized Christian to implement to some degree, according to their vocational commitments. Jesus is the model exemplar in His proclamation of the Good News and for living and serving in the Kingdom of God.

The notion of discipleship is used in Scripture with various meanings. In this study the use of the word is identified as a vocational commitment and call by Jesus to directly participate in partnership with Him in establishing and building the Kingdom of God on earth, and undertaking the ministries and the mission of evangelization which will achieve this goal. Understanding this notion of discipleship is central in an inter-play with the realities of the Mystery of the person of Christ and the dynamic life of living and serving in the Kingdom of God.

The notion of the Kingdom of God is directly or indirectly mentioned many times by Jesus Himself. Even his frequent use of parables to teach presupposes that His hearers are being enlightened by the Holy Spirit, who induces their ability to grasp the meaning of what Jesus is teaching through an inspired faith. Those hearers with hardness of heart just don't get what Jesus is saying about the revelation and truth of life in the Kingdom of God and may be following him for other reasons. The inspiration to accept the principles of discipleship, especially core commitment to discipleship, is revealed in the mystery, knowledge, and commitment to the Person of Christ through the gift of one's personal faith given in different portions. And Jesus says, "... *they will not understand, and I cannot heal them*" (Matthew 13: 15). This reality is hugely evident in the event presented in John Chapter 6, where Jesus reveals the doctrine of the Eucharist. Many of His disciples said, "*this is a hard saying*" (John 6:60), and no longer followed Him. In great sadness, Jesus asked his core of disciples, "*are you going to leave me also?*" (John 6:67).

114

The cost of discipleship is high. *"Whoever loves father or mother more than Me is not worthy of Me, and whoever loves son or daughter more than Me is not worthy of Me; and whoever does not take up his cross and follow after Me is not worthy of Me. Whoever finds his life will lose it, and whoever loses his life for My sake will find it"* (Matthew 10: 37-39). In the Word of God, what does it mean to deny self, give up self, or lose one's life? In viewing this reality Paul in the Galatians writes, *"I have been crucified with Christ; yet I live, no longer I, but Christ lives in me, in so far as I now live in the flesh, I live by faith in the Son of God who has loved me and given Himself up for me"* (Galatians 2:19-20). Jesus and Paul are not talking about a total annihilation of one's physical self as a person, but a radical transformation of my complete personhood to live as a new man or woman in Christ, and to give my total life, my physical life if necessary, for Christ, the Gospel, and the life of the Kingdom of God.

Considering this reality of the total gift of self in another way, Paul writes in Romans, *"I urge you therefore, brothers and sisters, by the mercy of God, to offer your bodies as a living sacrifice, holy and pleasing to God, your spiritual worship. Do not conform yourselves to this age but be transformed by the renewal of your mind, that you may discern what is the will of God, what is good and pleasing and perfect"* (Romans 12:1-2). Finally in Ephesians, *"as truth is in Jesus, that you should put away the old self of your former way of life, corrupted through deceitful desires, and be renewed in the spirit of your minds, and put on the new self, created in God's way in righteousness and holiness of truth"* (Ephesians 4: 22). We who wish to follow Christ must surrender as the Lord calls and gradually grow in discipleship in order to live totally and completely in the Divine Will.

All are called to some form of discipleship, configured to some degree in the Word. However, sometimes some are called in a heroic manner. We are reminded of this fact by the canonization of Mother Teresa of Calcutta. Another outstanding witness of costly grace and radical discipleship is an evangelical pastor, Dietrich Bonhoeffer. Once he came to see that Nazism in Germany was rooted in a national hatred and betrayal of God and a total annihilation of Jews and Christians, he joined the underground resistance which he had hesitated to do prior to this point. He understood that a reasonable revolution to defeat the evil political leadership in Germany was impossible. Bonhoeffer was eventually arrested by the Nazis and put in prison. He was hung two weeks before the Berlin liberation by the Americans. In his little book entitled, The Cost of Discipleship, he presents the distinction between **cheap grace and costly grace.**

Today, in our Christian world we are dealing with, for want of better word, a watered-down attitude in living the Christian life. For the most part, this is an unconscious attitude or convenient dissociation experienced by many individuals for various reasons even though they may believe in Christ and the Church to some degree. This attitude tends to express itself in a listless, weary feeling in one's attitude and expression of a faithful commitment and life-style. Such people may feel a distance in their relationship with God, and may regularly attend church and pray a little, but really exercise a secular humanistic and worldly attitude in their daily choices and decisions.

Bonhoeffer calls this ethos cheap grace. Such an approach could affect their conscience, causing them to dissociate from injustices of a personal and a social nature. They may not recognize certain types of moral evil, or experience an indifference to various negative and destructive social pathologies; for example, abortion, drugs, alcohol, prostitution, sex trafficking and pornography. Cheap Grace would also identify believers who would look to receive all the promises of God without exercising the costly grace of a loving fidelity. The narcissistic "culture of me-ism" influences faith oriented responses and moral decisions. It seems many Christians in America need to undertake a profound spiritual conversion and transformation in order to restore the freedom and dignity God has bestowed on them. The way forward requires a conversion from an addicted self-centeredness. This results in a decided movement toward spiritual maturity.

Chapter Fourteen

The Vision and Mission of a Disciple: Evangelization

Vision: *"Go into the whole world and proclaim the Gospel of grace, the Good News, the Gospel of the Kingdom to every creature"* (Mark 16:15). *"With great power the apostles bore witness to the Resurrection of Jesus, and great favor was accorded them all"* (Acts 4:33). *"When they saw him they worshiped him. Then Jesus approached and said to them, "All power in heaven and on earth has been given to me. Go, therefore, and make disciples of all nations, baptizing them in the name of the Father, and of the Son, and of the Holy Spirit, teaching them to observe all that I have commanded you. And behold, I am with you always, until the end of the age"* (Matthew 28:17-20). The Church is asking us in this age to reach out and undertake new efforts of evangelization, together with a real and practical openness to work with and serve with other Christian brothers and sisters.

At a certain point in the process of the experience of the **Grace of the Renewal** there will be a need to set up little "pockets" of formation, which will provide the inspiration and teaching for one to live out and be formed by the Word. This is a process of transformation in those things necessary

119

to inspire the changes in one's life which will call forth mature growth from a renewed and committed Christian. When people are searching for new life and truth, they usually show some degree of interest in those things that can bring desired growth in their lives. Opportunities which can at least start to fulfill these interests and desires is a good thing to consider. Therefore, a well-prepared program to lead and assist them to receive meaningful opportunities is most helpful. Participation in small group faith sharing is useful for spiritual growth and service. It is clear that most of us have busy schedules, and have little time for additional commitment. One of the greatest needs in this time of renewal is for some kind of ongoing spiritual growth and formation, designed to meet the needs of individuals who have little extra time.

There are a number of good groups in the Church which encourage some degree of discipleship and formation. Any such group should focus on three powers: The power in the Holy Spirit, the transforming power of the Cross, and the glorious experience of living in the power of the Resurrection. These three powers existing in a group's formation and discipleship preparation would ensure quality opportunities for growth.

The Church's Grace of the Renewal is a description of a three-fold actualizing empowerment of divine grace, plus the power of the Cross and the transforming peace and power of Jesus given to us by the grace of the glorious new life of the Resurrection. In this experience we not only know the enhanced activity of the grace and gifts of the Holy Spirit, but also the transforming power of Crucified Love on the Cross, and the grace and power of the Risen life experienced by living in the New Creation, becoming radically a new man and woman in Christ. This reality is and should be understood as one unifying operation and activity of grace. This dynamic is at the heart of one's practical training in evangelizing. This approach would keep before our eyes the commitment of becoming a disciple, a missionary, and a saint. To this point we would consider a refresher program in the life, power, and the gifts of the Holy Spirit as useful for practical evangelization.

Let us look at the notion of **personal evangelization.** Catholics are generally very afraid to undertake direct and personal evangelization. Two common reasons are that they believe that they do not know their faith very well, and many feel an inadequacy rooted in fear about sharing themselves and their personal experience of faith. Also, some do not have the call or gifts for personal evangelization. Faith sharing includes both personal experience of the Lord, and experiential knowledge of doctrine; not simply intellectual knowledge of doctrine. In the previous pages I attempted to suggest where special topics may be presented in programs, which would provide opportunities for teaching and training individuals to join in evangelization efforts and learn about other related areas. Seminars, days of recollection and renewal, and various types of teaching may be useful tools as well. Along with these things I also suggested supportive tools for healing and specific plans for growth in personal holiness. These possibilities can happen only if one is thirsty to drink at the well of the **Church's Grace of the Renewal.**

Again, we are highlighting various degrees of discipleship. These endeavors always begin slowly, and need to be undertaken with careful discernment and prayerful evaluation.

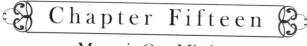

Chapter Fifteen

Mercy is Our Mission

The first things to consider are the charisms which empower merciful Christians, both the fellowship groups and each individual. Charisms were considered earlier in this work. All charisms are rooted in the context of Divine Love. Covenant Love is the key reality of God's grace bestowed in this season of Mercy. The heart of the gift is the Power of the Crucified One, the Victim of Love, Jesus, who expresses himself in a special way as Crucified Mercy, a mercy that infuses the four evangelical values:

1) Lifegiving Spirit-filled repentance as on going conversion and reconciliation.
2) Within the gift and dynamism of contemplation. A life of prayer, intercession, and atonement.
3) Living a lifestyle of spiritual poverty expressed through simplicity.
4) Rejoice in living in the Truth, and growing in humility.

Those who are called become witnesses of the Resurrection of Jesus; they are conscious of living in the New Creation. Those who desire to grow toward the goal to become merciful penitents are prayer warriors who intercede and aid others in growing in holiness. They are disciples of the Lord and servants of the mission; praying daily and practicing the spiritual and corporal works of mercy. They eventually become simple penitents who give their love away, give their lives away, and give their deaths away in generous atonement and love for the Father and their brothers and sisters in Jesus.

When we are united in Jesus to God as Father, in God as Father of the human family; in a real sense reconciliation with others. When we are united with one another with God as Father, we have a deep awareness of belonging; for we abide in the Father's Heart.

These four dispositional values are in union with the four mission values of servanthood. Both sets of values are one in living out the evangelical call to holiness in relationship in community. The four mission values may be identified as follows: The first is a **gift of creation**, where one is willing to participate in action which leads to constructively attempting to bring change to some of the challenging needs and issues that have emerged in today's global society. The second is **compassion**, which is the call to practice the corporal and spiritual works of mercy in available opportunities. The third is a commitment, under the guidance of the Holy Spirit, to participate in various communal relationships or associations designed to accomplish various works of mercy, **the mission of building community**. And the fourth is **becoming a peacemaker,** by making a commitment to grow in peacemaking in all the areas of one's life, relationships, and service.

The Mission of Peace: God wants us to be peace loving and of one mind and heart. As His sons and daughters, we are to abide in peace. God does not receive the sacrifice of one who lives in unjust conflict. We seek reconciliation with others, that God too may be appeased by our prayers because we are at peace. When we are united with one another in God, we have a deep awareness of belonging to one human family. **Peacemaking is making relationships right and just in the spirit of compassionate mercy.**

The action of peace involves people beyond our circle of friends. This is what makes peacemaking a very challenging mission. It is a matter of serving in mercy and working for true justice, especially for those on the margins of society, and possessing a willingness to sacrifice and embrace the cost. Even the most intimate bonds of friendship and the closest affinity of minds cannot lay true claim to this peace if they are not in agreement with the will of God.[35] Alliances, treaties, agreements, and governmental laws based on evil or worldly desires, covenants of crime, and pacts of vice—all lie outside the scope of this peace. Those who keep God ever in their hearts, and are anxious to preserve the unity of the Spirit in the bonds of peace, are true peace makers in the Father's will, in the affairs of life and in the world.[36]

The peace that Jesus brought to his disciples on the night of the Resurrection, which he gave to them twice, was a risen power-centered peace. **"Peace be with you.'** *When he said this he showed then his hands and side...Jesus said to them again.* **'peace be with you.'** *As the Father has sent me, so I send you, and when he had said this he breathed on them and said to them, Receive the Holy Spirit"* (John 20: 19b-21). This peace is a **word of power!** It designates good order, harmony, and the gift of completion. Right before that he showed them his wounds. The empowerment of Jesus's paschal accomplishment becomes a witness and commission to go forth and give this gift to others. Notice the power is a three-fold power as one empowerment: cross, resurrection and Spirit. This peace cannot be bestowed by human ingenuity, but is given by the Resurrected One as an empowerment peace and fruit of the Holy Spirit. This peace brings a state of joy, interior

---

35   St. Cyprian, Liturgy of the Hours, Vol. III, p. 377 (35?)

36   Liturgy of the Hours, Vol. III, Pope Leo The Great, p. 226

calm, communion with God, and a harmonious relationship with others. Our mission of peacemaking comes after we let God bring us empowerment, purity of heart, and risen faith. Minorite, humble pacemakers are aflame with charity in their hearts. A good and peaceful person turns all things to good.

Concrete Universal Principles of Action: In order for us to relate to practical adventures of peacemaking, we need to be exposed to a universal vision for the truth of peace. Pope John Paul II sponsored a peace dialogue in Assisi to which over 200 representatives of all the faiths of the world gathered in 1986 to dialogue and pray in regard to a commitment to work for world peace. The following are their ten statements of commitment they created for the advance of world peace.

- We commit ourselves to proclaiming our firm conviction that violence and terrorism are opposed to all true religious spirit, and we condemn all recourse to violence and war in the name of God and religion. We undertake to do everything possible to eradicate the causes of terrorism.
- We commit ourselves to educate people about respect and mutual esteem in order to achieve peaceful coexistence and solidarity among members of different ethnic groups, cultures and religions.
- We commit ourselves to promote the culture of dialogue so that understanding and trust may develop among individual and peoples as these are the conditions of authentic peace.
- We commit ourselves to defend the right of all human beings to lead a dignified life, in accordance with their cultural identity.
- We commit ourselves to engage in dialogue with sincerity and patience without considering

what separates us as an insurmountable wall; on the contrary, recognizing that facing our differences can become an occasion for greater reciprocal understanding.

- We commit ourselves to pardon each other's errors and prejudices of the past and present, and to support one another in the common struggle against egoism and abuses, hatred and violence, and in order to learn from the past that peace without justice is no true peace.
- We commit ourselves to stand at the side of those who suffer poverty and abandonment, speaking out for those who have no voice and taking concrete action to overcome such situations, in the conviction that no one can be happy alone.
- We commit ourselves to make our own the cry of those who do not surrender to violence and evil, and we wish to contribute with all our strength to give a real hope of the justice and peace to the humanity of our time.
- We commit ourselves to encourage all initiatives that promote friendship between peoples, in the conviction that, if a solid understanding between peoples is lacking, technological progress exposes the world to increasing dangers of destruction and death.
- We commit ourselves to ask the leaders of nations to make every possible effort to so as to build, at both national and international levels, a world of solidarity and peace founded on justice.[37]

---

37   Peace Dialogue in Assisi, *"Concrete Principles of Action: Peace Dialogue in Assisi."*, Pope John Paul II, October, 1986

Therefore, peacemakers are those who by patience, love, and gentle mercy are willing to choose between love and hatred and do many forms of judicious interventions, and spread their own inward peace about them for others.

The Gift of Creation: *"For creation awaits with eager expectation the revelation of the children of God; for creation was made subject to futility, not of its own accord but because of the one who subjected it, in hope that creation itself would be set free from slavery to corruption and would share in the glorious freedom of the children of God"* (Romans 8:19-21). It is the creative outpouring of His abundant goodness and love, which is the Life of God. Everything that is, including the whole universe, is a pure gift. All creation bears the imprint of God and points us to God. Some say that God's goal was always the Incarnation, and not just a loving plan for our salvation. *"In all wisdom and insight, He has made known to us the mystery of His will in accord with His favor that he set forth in Him as a plan for the fullness of times, to sum up all things in Christ, in heaven and on earth"* (Ephesians 1: 8b-10). In Colossians, we read that the preeminence or the primacy of Christ is so beautifully stated, *"He is the image of the invisible God, the first born of all creation. For in Him were created all things in heaven and on earth, the visible and the invisible…all things were created through Him and for Him. He is before all things, and in him all things hold together. He is the head of the body, the Church. He is the beginning, the first born from the dead, in all things that He Himself might be preeminent. For in Him all the fullness was pleased to dwell, and through Him to reconcile all things for Him, making peace by the blood of His cross, whether those on earth or those in heaven"* (Colossians. 1: 15-20). For Francis of Assisi the entire universe, all of creation, is a beautiful manifestation of God. In Francis' world, all of creation and everything that exists has value because it is from God, revealed in and through Christ. We should also have a contemplative gaze which transforms our whole life, and especially in doing the mission. We come alive to God's presence and generosity in and through creation, and embrace a constant state of gratitude. This means having a dependency on God's action in the world where we may see the simplest things as gift and respond with joy and praise.[38] Today we generally show little reverence for creation; most of us take it for granted. Many in America and elsewhere live in abundant affluence. Affluence can cause us to become preoccupied and obsessed with possession, withholding, keeping, accumulating, and developing. Because of this, we lose that sense of giftedness, gratitude, and dependency. Filled with attitudes of anxiety, fear and unfilled objectives, we easily lose that sense of dependency on God which enables us to live freely and joyfully in our world. We are sated with what cannot satisfy or sustain us; we are consumed by consumerism. The rediscovery of the gifts of dependency, gratitude, generosity, joy, and peace what flows from these values is an essential attitude which we need to sustain us. The global future will be unsustainable without it.[39]

Modern science is demonstrating how connected we are to all things. We cannot exist alone; we are relational and social beings. We recognize the growing pace of globalization, yet often our actual experience is one of disconnectedness and isolation. We have become obsessed with comfort and technology, which has contributed to losing to some degree real communication in relationships. Given these conditions, there is also some awareness of humanity rushing forward in a conflicting and complicated path of disorientation; a destructive process of neglect, abuse, and materialistic greed, where creatures are out of harmony with one another, and see no purpose in life other than self-fulfillment and self-satisfaction. Our present ecological crisis has to do with our

---

38   A Franciscan View of Creation, *"Wisdom For a World Going Mad"*, Lecture, Br. Samuel, SSF
39   Ibid., in the lecture

failure to acknowledge God's plan for all creation. If what we are doing now continues, we will not be able to sustain our existence and respond to and fulfill the good things God wants to do for humanity and the fulfillment of his plan of love. **It has become obvious that we need to respond to a call of repentance. It is only by expressing penitence for our abuse of creation,** and by a fundamental change in the perception of our place and purpose in the world that we can be brought back into true relationship with each other and with our creation. The task of the Church would be to offer praise and worship back to God, heal resistance, and respond to a necessary call for repentance as we redirect our relationship with ourselves and with each other.[40]

Pope John Paul II articulated new ethical duties for Catholics, indeed for the whole human family. He described the environmental crisis as rooted in a moral crisis for humanity, caused by selfishness and sin, and our lack of respect for life. He stated that humanity should explore, examine, and safeguard the integrity of creation. He presented duties for human individuals and institutions of all kinds: the nations of the world should cooperate in the management of the earth's goods, individual nations should care for their citizens, and individuals undertake an education in ecological responsibility. Pope Benedict XVI continued to elaborate theological and ethical rationales for protecting the environment. He emphasized the importance of listening to the "voice of the earth." Creation, thus has theological and moral significance, for it provides lessons for us to understand our existence and purpose here on earth, and calls for dialogue with contemporary ethics, science, and public policy. We need to be awakened to the communion of life that we share with all creation, and deeply appreciate that we are one family in a dynamic relationship with all facets of creation. It is important for us to see that we are creatures of God, living in relationship to our Creator

40   Ibid., in the lecture

and creation according to the gospel. Our responsibility is to love God, and our love of creation emerges from this love.[41]

All of creation makes known the Creator; the power, goodness, and wisdom of God shines through in all creatures. In this dynamic setting, Divine life in creation is like a river that flows from the spring of God spreading across the land to purify and fructify it, and returning all the individual components of creation back to the glory of God. As we learn and understand more about God, we come to recognize His love in creation. Every creature, not only humans, reflects to some degree God's handiwork, and the rich diversity of creatures reflects the depth and richness of God. God becoming man reflects the beginning of the transfiguration and transformation of all creation in the universe, specifically in this world. The Word revealed in the Scriptures shows the transforming power and love in the cross of Christ revealed through the Incarnation. At the most fundamental level our origin is God and our destiny is God. Our challenge is to live with an awareness, of this awesome, superabundant love of God, expressed so vividly through creation. The Incarnation as the foremost expression of God's love is the most important reality in the cosmos. The Son is first in God's intention to love and thus create. The divine desire to become incarnate was integral and intrinsic to the divine plan, and creation was made capable of bearing Christ in incarnate form. Creation was created for the Incarnation.[42]

Pope Francis spoke about this when he addressed this timely topic. He pointed out that Pope Benedict encouraged us to learn how to listen to "the voice of the earth," to grasp the

---

41   Pope John Paul II, "The Ecological Crisis: "A Common Responsibility, 1990 World Day of Peace Message

42   *Franciscan View of Creation: The Moral Significance of Creation in the Franciscan Theological Tradition: Implication for Contemporary Catholics and Public Policy,* Essay by Keith Douglas Warner, OFM, pp. 40-46

rhythm and logic of creation, and encourages us to respect and listen to creation as a free gift. Pope Francis uses the example of a farmer in regard to the care and cultivation of the land. He mentions that we often neglect and exploit the environment, often driven by pride of domination and possession. We do not consider creation a free gift, the goods of the earth which we must be responsible for. Why does this happen? He maintains it happens because we have moved away from God. To cultivate and care encompasses not only the relationship to the material creation, but also applies to human relationships. The Popes have spoken that we are living in a time of crisis. We are in serious danger; we see this in the environment, but above all we see this in human persons. This is not a superficial problem but a profound problem, Human ecology is in serious danger because the cause is profound. Environmental ecology and human ecology go together. It is impossible to separate them. Pope Francis gave numerous examples of individuals who are unjustly suffering because of the way the human community is engaging more and more in a culture of waste and neglect of the suffering poor.[43]

The Church has stressed this fact many times, and many people say that is true, but the system continues as before because it is dominated by the dynamics of the world economy and finance. Man is not in charge today money is in charge. Men and women are sacrificed to the idol of profit. This culture of waste tends to become the common value. People are disposed of as though they are trash. That infects everyone—human life, old people, the disabled, the sick, etc. The human person is no longer perceived as the primary value to be respected and protected, beyond economic parameters. While all over the world many are starving and malnourished, we have become used to excess of food and other resources, and

---

43   Pope Francis' general audience in St. Peters Square, on the occasion of the UN World Environment Day

so we waste so much food. Whenever we throw away food we are stealing from the poor. When food is shared in a fair way with solidarity, every community can meet the needs of the poorest.[44]

Pope Francis invites us to action in regard to changing our practices in regard to the misuse and unjust distribution of our resources, and to take positive action in regard to overcoming this problem for the sake of the entire human family. He asks us to be attentive to every person, make a commitment to respect creation, and work to overcome the culture of waste and disposal and promote a culture of solidarity.

What we have learned over the past fifty years or so is that environmental problems and the care of creation is a complex reality. Scientific study, ethics, policy and other endeavors are necessary. Religious communities and other church associations need to play a more active role in environmental issues, and of course the concerted activity of responsible individual efforts is crucial.

---

44   Ibid., UN World Environment Day

Part III

Chapter One

Penitents of Mercy:
Resurgence of Penitential Life in the Church

The grace of the Holy Spirit is bringing about in the Church today a resurgence, a call, an invitation for individuals who are ready, to live in a new way the penitential life within the tradition of the Church. The condition of the world today in which we live is rapidly developing into a neo-pagan society. Secular humanism has infiltrated every dimension of modern and post-modern life. Narcissistic individualism is expressed everywhere. All one needs to do is turn on the television to witness this reality.

Those who buy into modern secularism consciously push the reality of God's involvement in human affairs to the outward margins of existence. Therefore, we are seeing an inevitable descent into barbarism, which is manifesting itself in all dimensions of human existence. Throughout history, when humans respond to God in this manner, He is forced to bring judgment on humankind, the nation, and the Church. However, along with his purifying judgment, God also manifests his powerful mercy for renewal, conversion, and reform. The Lord pours out his merciful love and calls those he loves to repentance and conversion, inviting them to embrace the Gospel, and embrace a penitential way of life.

Many of the specific actions and unique graces of the Holy Spirit's action today are calling Catholics and other Christians to live new forms of the penitential life. There are various ways of viewing the penitential life. However, here is one attempt at a definition: It is an evangelical grace which entails major interior transformation and a visible change in the structure of one's external behaviors and life-style. It invites us to take the time and seriously evaluate our values and principles in relationship to the attitudes and teaching of Jesus in the Gospel, the authentic teaching of the Church, and in the current action of the Spirit in the Church and in our society. This demanding approach will call for a sorting out of "the bad from the good." This exercise could well lead to a significant change in the way we live, or at least some adjustment. This process usually invites identifying the strengths, the values, and the good things upon which our life and faith is founded, and identifying any behavior that undermines a holy, devoted, and zealous Christian life. We should not be so foolish as to try changing all negative issues at one time. A wiser and hopefully successful approach is to change one thing at a time. A period of life-giving and Spirit-filled repentance may for some be a good way to make a start.

⚭ Chapter Two ⚭

The Influence of the Penitential Movement
in the History of the Church

The penitential movement gradually emerged in the life of the Church somewhere at the end of the 10th Century. It was a time when drastic spiritual renewal and structural reform was needed in the Church. When St. Francis of Assisi arrived on the scene, the penitential movement had been underway for over a hundred and fifty years. Therefore, in a sense, St. Francis joined something that was slowly making headway in the life of the Church. He and others, under the power and guidance of the Holy Spirit, expanded the movement in a major manner. It may be helpful for us, in terms of understanding the penitential movement, to briefly review how it happened for him.

Francis Bernadone lived a very worldly life in Assisi until his later teenage years. He was ambitious for worldly success and desired great fame as a knight. His father, a wealthy merchant who desired wealth and a higher civic status, supported Francis' imaginary and idealistic goals. Just at that time Assisi declared war on Perugia, a larger town about forty miles northwest of Assisi. Francis, decked out in the military finery of the time, joined the nobles from Assisi in an attack on the Perugians. In the midst of the battle Francis was captured and spent a miserable year in a dungeon prison until he was ransomed by his father. He presented a joyful spirit among the prisoners from Assisi who had been captured, but eventually his health was broken and he returned to Assisi a very broken and sick person.

Still Francis was not satisfied. After he recovered from illness he tried again. He met an old scarred knight who had only battered and insufficient equipment. Inspired by the Holy Spirit who was working quietly in Francis's soul, he gave his horse and equipment to the old knight. He returned to Assisi in disgrace to deal with his father's rage. Francis took up work in his father's shop, and from time to time he would give money and material goods to the poor. This practice also incurred his father's ire. The Holy Spirit now moved more powerfully in the heart of Francis, deepening his compassion and a strong desire for prayer. Eventually Francis and a friend frequently spent time in the caves above Assisi in prayer. One day, after six hours in prayer, Francis had a life-size vision of Jesus hanging on the Cross. His heart was pierced with compassion, and ever after when Jesus Crucified was mentioned, Francis would break into tears.[45] Francis' heart was pierced with the gift of Divine mercy and compassion.

However, Francis was not yet a completely converted man, nor had he finally left the "world." He was still hanging on to his father's wealth. Shortly after the vision of Jesus Crucified, he was riding a horse on the plains of Assisi, as the legend holds, when his horse was startled, and Francis beheld the presence of a disfigured leper standing in front of him. The refined nature of Francis blanched at the sight of the poor leper. He wheeled his horse around to flee, but the Holy Spirit moved him with deep compassion, **compassion-evoking**

---

45   Recorded in The Major Life of St. Francis by Bonaventure

love power (CELP). He jumped off his horse and embraced the leper and kissed him. Just as quickly, the leper was gone. The legend has it that the leper was Christ. Francis himself states in his writings that his experience was a major turning point in his conversion as a penitent; after lingering for a little while, he **finally left the world.**

The highlights in the conversion story of Francis can be similar to what happens in our own conversions, though usually not as dramatic as his and some other saints.

Some of these features in need of grace-filled conversion could be as follows:

1. Intense worldly ambition.
2. Seeking after immediate sensual pleasure.
3. Making bad choices in relationships and sometimes paying the price.
4. Discouragement and depression because of significant failures and brokenness (spiritual, moral, emotional, practical failures and major losses etc.). Whether or not these things have happened to us, we may still be attached to the things of this world. To live the life of a penitent, one must move to truly leave the "world."

After leaving "the world", Francis felt a deep need to serve by doing mercy work. An old priest lived in a broken-down chapel called San Damian, right outside of the gates of Assisi. He was using his father's money to buy stone to rebuild the chapel. One day when he was working in the chapel in front of the altar he looked up at the image of Christ on the Cross, and Jesus spoke to him: "Francis go and rebuild my Church." Even though he misunderstood and kept rebuilding broken down chapels around Assisi, he now had a mission. These incidents led to a total break with his father, which led him to exclaim that God in heaven was now his only Father. His initial conversion was now complete. Others then moved to join him in living the new life of an evangelical penitent within the Church.

Another example of one called to the penitential life is St. Rose of Lima. St. Rose was a member of a large and poor family. She experienced a tremendous desire for prayer and contemplation. Her father built a prayer shack in the back of their property. In view of the fact that Rose was extremely beautiful, her family naturally expected her to marry one of the many wealthy men seeking her hand. There was significant pressure on her to say yes to one of them. However, Rose felt a strong call to remain single and dedicate her life to contemplation. In order to ward off her suitors, she sprinkled hot pepper on her face and made herself pockmarked.

Rose literally spent hours in her prayer shack. The Lord bestowed the gift of contemplation and other magnificent mystical graces upon her. She had a vision that she traveled over the whole world proclaiming how magnificent and tremendous the life of grace was for all Christians.[46] Rose also told them to embrace all the suffering and affliction of their lives, because after those crosses came an infinite abundance of grace. And in this grace was found the transforming power and love of one's eternal union with God. She even went so far to say that if we understood these marvelous gifts of love, we would seek out affliction and suffering.

Here is another account of one of her miracles: One night, her father asked her brother to go downstairs to the basement and get some bread from the cupboard. Her brother told everyone that there was nothing in the cupboard. Rose said that there was bread there; her father told her brother to check again. He came upstairs with a huge loaf of bread, enough for the whole family.

St. Rose of Lima made several attempts at entering religious life, but these proved unsuccessful for various reasons. She

---

46   The Liturgical Feast of St. Rose of Lima, August 23rd, vol. IV, pp. 1341-1343

was a friend of St. Martin de Porres, a Dominican brother. Both of them served the black slaves being brought over from Africa until the two were completely exhausted. They were both famous in the City for the generous service of the poor. Rose eventually left her family and moved in with a couple who were friends of hers. In the last four years of her life, exhausted from long hours in prayer, intense suffering, and generous care of the poor, she wasted away and died at the young age of 31, one of the most famous penitents in the Church.

The principles of evangelical discipleship ought to be applied to every baptized Christian, because they dynamically represent the heart of the Gospel. It seems, however, that it is not necessary for every baptized Christian to be trained into a formal core of disciples in order to receive salvation, gain sanctification, and serve in the mission of the Church. This understanding indicates that the values of discipleship make up what could be termed **the normative Christian life.** Yet in the history of the Church there are different calls, and by the grace of the Holy Spirit some are called to "much more" in their life and service in the Church. This does not necessarily mean that these individuals are better than others, holier, or especially pleasing to God. However, it does mean that these individuals are configured in a special manner with additional graces of penance. Generally speaking, all are called to do penance in their individual Christian life, but some people are called to a unique configuration which others are not necessarily invited to undertake. Therefore, some are called by the Lord to live a complete life-style as a **Penitent.** In the following pages, we will describe more fully what it specifically may mean to be called by grace to be a **Penitent.**

The call and life of **Servants of Mercy** who are missionary disciples, subsequently penitents, receive the grace and its transforming power from the blood and water flowing from the heart of the Crucified One. The Father's gift of mercy reveals his love and riches in the glory of his Son. This transforming gift of **Crucified Mercy** enables one to surrender himself in a process of evangelical conversion induced by reform, reconciliation, and sanctification. These graces generate an experience of Spirit-filled and life-giving repentance, which enables one to enjoy a deep sense of gratitude, glory, and praise while embracing the evangelical mission of the Church, and leading others into the glorious life of the Kingdom as **mercy-filled penitents.**

What sort of design would a penitential life-style among zealous Christians look like today? Generally, we could say that a penitent is one who is faithful to the Father's mercy, living a distinct way of life in a practical situation in order to manifest and witness to the Gospel and lead others to the life of the Kingdom. This ethos is usually best expressed in some form of flexible association or fraternity dedicated to the mission.

Jesus is the Glorified Lamb of God of the New Creation: He comes to do the Father's will, and take away our sin. Energized by the power of the Spirit and responding in heroic love, He is baptized in the Holy Spirit, transformed in the fire of the Holy Spirit, and as the Father's Son, the servant who embraces the saving suffering for humanity. For those called to a penitential way of life the **basic charism is Crucified Love and Mercy.** The Crucified One embodies the fulfillment of the Father's mission by definitively establishing the reality of the **New Creation.** Therefore, Jesus is identified as the Perfect One of the New Creation. *"So whoever is in Christ is a new creation"* (2 Corinthians 5:17), and *"we implore you on behalf of Christ be reconciled to God"* (2 Corinthians 5:20). *"Those who live might no longer live for themselves but for him who for their sake died and was raised"* (2 Corinthians 5:15). *"Now the Lord is the Spirit, and where the Spirit of the*

Lord is there is freedom. All of us gazing with unveiled faces on the glory of the Lord are being transformed into the same image from glory to glory, as from the Lord who is the Spirit" (2 Corinthians 3: 17-18).

The call to be evangelical penitents requires a particular spirituality where the values of the Gospel are lived in semi-heroic fashion. **Crucified Mercy** is a powerful charism of penance that demands living a life of evangelical conversion by those who are **Servants of Mercy.** These charisms are gifts of love from the Father in Jesus which gives the penitents special power, life, and wisdom for loving and serving others. Healing flows from the corporal and spiritual works of mercy. The servants of mercy living a penitential spirituality become missionary disciples who freely embrace a **seraphic spirituality,** which is the dynamism of divine and heavenly love flowing from a union with the Lord, who is Incarnate Crucified Mercy. The source of merciful love, which the servant of Mercy experiences, flows from the Father's heart as rivers of grace-filled mercy, a gift of Covenant Love poured out for the healing and salvation of all. The pierced heart of the humbled and poor Christ becomes the center of knowledge of Crucified Love, and the dynamic power of contemplating this truth invites Servants of Mercy more deeply into a fruitful union of being mercy-full penitents. These Spirit-given graces support a life of virtue and service. The mercy of God is poured out into the hearts of the brothers and sisters who are poor servants of His charity rooted in mercy. These *penitents* grow toward being **Servants of Mercy who are Missionary Disciples of Atonement. In short, they are Merciful Penitents living in a time of spiritual renewal and reform.**

What matters more than anything else in a basic sense for a penitent is the dynamic truth of living the Gospel in the **New Creation.** *"So whoever is in Christ is a new creation: the old things have passed away; behold new things have come. And* *all this is from God, who has reconciled us to himself through thirst"* (2 Corinthians 5:17). In the **New Creation,** the veil which covers our faces, which keeps us from seeing the glory of the Lord is removed. Because all of us gazing with unveiled faces on the glory of the Lord are being transformed gradually into his image. The way in which this reality is to transpire is to have faith that God in His infinite Mercy and in His plan for salvation has sent His Son to be lifted up as a sacrifice for our sin. The Cross is the means of our salvation. *"Yet it was our infirmities that He bore, our sufferings that He endured, while we thought of Him as one stricken as one smitten by God and afflicted. But He was pierced for our offences and crushed for our sins. Upon Him was the chastisement that makes us whole, by His stripes we were healed"* (Isaiah 53:4-5). The offering of Jesus' life on the Cross brings us, once and for all, the forgiveness of sin and the merit of salvation. We are redeemed by the blood of Christ," *"That you were ransomed from your futile conduct not with perishable things like gold or silver, but with* **the precious blood of Christ** *as of a spotless unblemished lamb"* (1 Peter 1:18-19). Therefore, He is always able to save those who approach God through Him, *"since He lives forever to make intercession for them"* (Hebrews 7:25). *"Who will condemn? It is Christ Jesus who died, rather raised to life, who also is at the right hand of God, who indeed intercedes for us"* (Romans 8:34). The Cross of Jesus Christ should not be emptied of its meaning: *"The message of the Cross is foolishness to those who are perishing, but to us who are being saved it is the power of God . . . Christ the power of God and the wisdom of God"* (1 Corinthians 1:18,24).

Because we are baptized into the death and resurrection of Christ through our own baptism, we are connected to Christ in an unbroken bond in His offering to the Father and His own intercession. In union with Jesus, we actually experience Christ's suffering in our own body: "Always carrying about in the body the dying of Jesus, so the life of Jesus may be manifested in our body. For we who live are being constantly given up to death for the sake of Jesus, so that the life of Jesus may be manifested in our mortal flesh" (2 Corinthians 4:10-11). In the mystery of this real and mystical union we rejoice, "Beloved, do not be surprised that a trial by fire is occurring among you, as if something strange were happening to you. But rejoice to the extent that you share in the sufferings of Christ, so that when his glory is revealed you may also rejoice exultantly" (1 Peter 4:13-14). This is what makes our dynamic union and suffering love in the Cross of Christ so fruitful. We become missionary disciples of suffering victims of love: *"That I might live for God. I have been crucified with Christ; yet I live, no longer I, but Christ lives in me; in so far as I now live in the flesh, I live by faith in the son of God who has loved me and given himself up for me"* (Galatians 2:19b-20). Our call as penitent missionaries of suffering: *"Now I rejoice in my sufferings for your sake, and in my flesh I am filling up what is lacking in the afflictions of Christ on behalf of his Body, which is the Church"* (Colossians 1:24). St. Paul makes an extraordinary statement here. How can anything be lacking in the ultimate sacrifice of Christ? What this means is that our sufferings have meaning power; united with the Cross, our sufferings can be offered, like Christ's, on behalf of the Church. We participate in the work of redemption. In the shadow of the Cross, all human suffering is a power filled with meaning, and we embrace that reality fully through a mission of Atonement.[47]

---

47   Commentary on Colossians, 1:24, translation of New American Bible

Chapter Three

A Spirituality of Merciful Penitents
The Call to Serve the Church as a Penitent

"The next day he saw Jesus coming toward him and declared: here is the Lamb of God who takes away the sin of the world! . . . The one who sent me to baptize with water said to me, He on whom you see the Spirit descend and remain is the one who baptizes with the Holy Spirit"

— John 1:29-34

In the Johannine account, Jesus is baptized in the midst of a powerful description of the ministry of John the Baptist. John was the Judean ascetic who preached repentance, conversion, reform, and baptized for the forgiveness of sin. John prepared the way for the mission and ministry of Jesus. Jesus embodied the fulfillment of the mission of John. This is the Jesus who appeared in a Nazarene synagogue and called for repentance and reform in the year of favor bestowed by the Lord. Here stands the beloved Son in whom the Father is well pleased. Jesus, who comes to do the Father's will of salvation, not only baptizes in the Holy Spirit and its transforming fire, but embodies in reconciliation the heart and fullness of the gospel. He is the Incarnate One, the perfect Lord of the New Creation (see Mark 1:14-15).

One of the objectives of this book is to invite individuals who are Christian to respond to the invitation to serve in the Church as **merciful penitents.** It is a grace-filled call to be a penitent, wherein the values of the gospel demand a particularized spirituality in which these values are lived in a generous fashion. A penitent is one who is a servant of the Lord's mercy, and a **Missionary Disciple of Atonement.** This is the **narrow way** which gives power, life, and wisdom about a special approach to living the Gospel as merciful penitent disciples. The servant of mercy spirituality is composed of special gifts called charisms which provide a unique expression and operation for one's life and service. A penitent is a person who responds to the invitation of the Crucified Merciful One. This reality entails a complete surrender to the power of the Cross and the new life and power of the Resurrection by the empowered grace of the Holy Spirit. Thus the penitent is consecrated, set apart for a mission of sacrifice, love, and mercy. The spirituality of merciful-filled penitents can be lived out in various forms or groups of shared relationships and services, which empower one to experience the fruits and blessings of penance as one deepens in this way of life.

There are a number of considerations to achieve these objectives. A clear approach to spiritual growth and healing will be necessary for one who wants to be a part of this endeavor. A solid commitment to personal sanctification and learning the ways and means of living the penitential life in the modern world would be primarily important. It is good to be aware that striving for personal holiness without generous service can lead to spiritual narcissism. Training in communication, faith sharing, praying for others, and personal evangelization is necessary to accomplish the mission of mercy. The experience of small group fellowships will demonstrate the joy of sharing and living the Gospel as merciful penitents. This way of life together will engage a constant growth in being a Missionary Disciple of Mercy and Atonement. The role of power-centered reparation and atonement rooted in reconciliation gives a primary focus to merciful penitents for doing the mission of employing God's abundant mercy on the world and in the Church, and on the specific undertakings of a penitent movement.

The call and fruitfulness of a penitent develops through various stages of change as God wills, as this will get practically revealed in one's life. A person's vocational decision is the principal shaping instrument on how a person lives out the call to be a penitent. We are currently witnessing in many ways that love has grown cold in our society. Something more is crucially necessary from generous people who want to live more than a normative Christian life. A grace-filled call to be a penitent reveals a special spirituality. The call presupposes that one receives a special gift of love from the Father in Jesus which gives power, life, and wisdom in living the Gospel Way of Life. We should not take lightly the necessity of receiving from the Lord a call and additional grace in this regard. When Joshua received the anointing from Moses, he realized he and the people needed to prepare for the new work the Lord had for them, which was taking possession of the Promised Land. Joshua proclaimed that he and his family would serve the Lord, and then he called for a renewal of the Covenant by the entire people. He realized that a special faithfulness and power was necessary for a new work. Joshua knew that new types of challenges and temptations would arise. He warned the Israelites that the Lord would turn against them if they were not faithful to Him and to the Covenant.

In the words of St. Francis of Assisi, "And all of us lesser brothers, useless servants, humbly ask and beg all those who wish to serve the Lord God . . . that all of us may preserve in the true faith and **in penance,** for otherwise no one will be saved. Let us all love the Lord God with all our heart, with all our soul, and with all our mind and with all our strength, and with fortitude and with total understanding, with all our powers, with every effort, with every affection, every emotion, every desire and every wish. He has given and gives to each one of us our whole body, our whole soul, and our whole life. He created us and redeemed us, **and will save us by his mercy alone."** This prayer of Francis is an inspired description of the Lord, truly a mystic's prayer and a wonderful description of the penitential life.[48]

Francis's and Clare's unique focus as penitents was the result of their appreciation for the gift of God's love revealed in the Incarnation. As penitents they concentrated their whole-hearted acceptance of the Gospel in the process of repentance, conversion, contemplation, and taking on a full life of penance. The Word became flesh manifested in Francis the enduring triune love of God in the person of Christ, and his unity and primacy in all of creation. The spirituality of Francis is called seraphic spirituality because of its emphasis on divine and heavenly love revealed in the person of Jesus. The goal of his **seraphic spirituality** is the contemplation and union (becoming one) with the Father in and through the Son, by the Holy Spirit (Trinitarian Oneness), *"Holy Father, keep them in your name that you have given me, so that they may be one just as we are . . . I pray not only for them, but also for those who will believe in me through their word, so that they may all be one, as you, Father are in me and I in you, that they*

---

48   The prayer of St. Francis of Assisi to do penance, Early Rule, chapter 15, No. 7-11, pp. 132-134

may also be in us, that the world may believe that you sent me. . . so that they may be one as we are one, I in them and you in me, that they may be brought to perfection as one, that the world may know that you sent me, and you love them as you love me" (John 17: 11-23). We receive this triune life and love from the person of Jesus.

Internal Elements: The source of the penitent's merciful love flows from the Father's heart as rivers of mercy. It is a gift to penitents in Covenant Love for the salvation of all. The path that a penitent is invited to choose is one of experiencing the endearing and enduring love in the humble person of Christ. The center of this dynamic union is a generous embrace of the poor Crucified One. It is embracing Crucified Love in the Heart of Jesus, the Shepherd King, who laid down His life for His sheep. Contemplatives in the midst of men, penitents, become one with him through contemplating the Pierced One, who is Risen and Glorified. Poor and lesser penitents fix their gaze on the face of our glorified King, and center in on Divine Love as missionary disciples of the Good Shepherd, who are Servants of Mercy. In other words, a person responds to the invitation of the Crucified Merciful One to become a penitent.

"We are constantly being handed over to death for Jesus' sake so that His life may be revealed in us" (2 Corinthians 4:11). Fully aware of the value of his sufferings and tribulations, St. Paul blesses God in the midst of his sufferings, and thanks Him as though he had bestowed a fine reward. He thinks it is an honor to be able to suffer for Christ, Who subjected himself to much shame in order to free us from the dreadful effects of sin. Jesus exalts us by giving us his Spirit and making us sons and daughters of God. He bestows on us in His own person and through His own efforts a proof and pledge of heavenly joy. As we share generously in the sufferings of Christ, so do we share generously in His consolation. This is the way Christ and His disciples have always traveled. He calls it the narrow

way, but it leads straight to life. God grant that our hearts may find no rest and seek no other food in this world, save in hardship and suffering in the Lord's Cross.[49] One is invited by the action of grace to personally and gradually surrender to the transforming power of the Cross. St. Paul expresses this clearly: *"Now I rejoice in my sufferings for your sake, and in my flesh I am filling up what is lacking in the afflictions of Christ on behalf of his body, which is the church"* (Colossians 1:24).

A penitent is one who understands this dynamic truth by the enlightenment of the Holy Spirit, as the gift of the Holy Spirit is poured out in the penitent's heart, and fills that person with a universal love of all. Thus the penitent is consecrated, set apart, for a mission of love; namely the spiritual means of reparation and atonement for the purpose of universal reconciliation, and bringing others to know and live in Christ. As a penitent grows in the love of the Cross, he or she experiences the fruit of reconciliation and peace. A penitent experiences the power of the Passion and Cross of Jesus in the gift of mercy. A penitent then seeks to identify with the One who loved him and gave His life for him. The penitent who is a servant of Mercy will gradually yearn to embrace the **kenosis** of a self-emptying love of the Son. This one desires to become poor and little and imitate the poor suffering Christ. In his book entitled *The Life of St. Clare* by Regis Armstrong, Cap., we read, "The Crucified took possession of the lover, and she was inflamed with such love of the mystery and power of the Cross, that it should be perfectly clear from this that the Tree of the Cross was planted in the breast of Clare; while its fruit refreshes the soul, its leaves externally provide healing."[50] The spirituality of the power of the Cross and the empowerment of the Risen Christ, which

---

49   *St. John of Avila, the Liturgy of the Hours,* vol. III, pp. 1826-1827

50   *Clare of Assisi* by Regis Armstrong, OFM, Cap. p. 220, No. 32, 35 Letter to the Entire Order, No. 27-29, p. 58

is characterized by His appearance in the Upper Room the night of the Resurrection (See John 20:19-23), is rooted in the experience of the Lord's Risen Power and Life; it is the same spirituality of true penitents who are servants of mercy.

Penitential spirituality is communitarian: A penitent servant of mercy lives to serve in various communal ways through the **Church's Grace of the Renewal**; the power of the Cross, the anointed empowerment of the Resurrection, and the infusion and operation of the graces of the Holy Spirit. The spirituality of mercy-filled penitents may be lived individually or in various forms or associations or some type of shared relationships. These rivers of mercy flow from the Father's heart through the heart of Jesus Christ. The stance of penitent servants of Mercy is one of being a missionary disciple. One stands before the Cross beholding the wounds of Christ, and gazes upon the glory of the face of Christ, the victorious Lamb. The penitent servants of Mercy, contemplatives in action in the midst of men, grow in union with Crucified Love and tend to be drawn into some form or appropriate association of relationships. The simple structures of communication and sharing are yet to emerge. The Spirit could eventually lead individuals to various types of flexible groups for those who experience a call to become a modern penitent.

Let us reflect on two aspects in the life of Francis of Assisi in relationship to two of the internal or spiritual elements in the spirituality of servants of mercy, who search or choose to become a penitent. First, in one's own personal life one may discern the call to be a penitent and then respond. The second is to pray, do penance and show mercy to others. Francis, it seems, wrote this letter to the entire Order toward the end of his life. At the end of the letter, in a beautiful prayer he reveals his heart to his brothers in a way which could characterize a similar response in our own hearts, if we want to give our all to Jesus: "Look, brothers, at the humility of God and pour out your hearts before Him! Humble yourselves, as well, that you may be exalted by Him. Therefore, hold back nothing of yourselves for yourselves so that he who gives Himself totally to you may receive you totally." Francis was led by God to a personal conversion through the practice of prayer and penance. As he began to do penance, he practiced mercy by serving the lepers, "I practiced mercy with them, and then I lingered a little while, and I finally left the "world."[51]

Individuals who practice these approaches of living the Gospel mature, as Francis did, into a permanent committed life of doing penance as a penitent. We certainly may not be called to the same life-style, but we are called **to be consecrated**, set apart, to be a penitent, and this necessitates some visible pattern of life. Viewing these matters from an external point of view, we need a framework or a flexible structure which provides a clear understanding for living a penitential way of life. The construct that Francis provided for those who desired to live a lay penitential life in the world was one of **servanthood.** As servants of mercy and missionary disciples, "be inwardly cleansed, interiorly enlightened, and inflamed by the fire of the Holy Spirit, so that we may be able to follow in the footsteps of the beloved Son, our Lord Jesus Christ"[52] The notion of Servanthood can only be fully appreciated within the ambient of a "fellowship" or a flexible fraternal format; it requires some expression of a relational pattern. Servanthood is idealized in Scripture in the image of Jesus, the Suffering Servant Son, prophetically presented in Scripture as the One who inaugurates salvation for humankind through His suffering and death. It is through His love by which He sanctifies humanity in which He is a member and for whom He is the only one who can represent them. In the New Testament, the Suffering Servant reveals more specifically His

51   Ibid., L Ord. n.51
52   Earlier Rule, c. 23, No. 37-38: Also in prayer of St. Francis before a Crucifix

role by washing His disciples' feet. A new unfolding of the notion of servant in John 13 which demonstrates the identity and role of a servant in the reign of God, Jesus performs this lowly and humbling service of foot washing for his disciples (John 13: 2b-11). He reminded them time and time again that he had come to serve and not to be served.

Jesus even went further in describing the lowliness that is characteristic of the servant of the Lord. When the disciples were arguing about who was the greatest in the Kingdom of God, they put this question to Him. He responded by calling a child to Him, placing it in their midst and said, *"Amen, I say to you unless you turn and become like children you will not enter the kingdom of heaven"* (Matthew 18: 3-4). Therefore, humility, lowliness, and littleness are essential features in the life and behavior of a penitent. Servanthood always becomes concrete in some form of relationships, which suggests that servanthood embraces some degree of the communal ideal.

In a penitential framework, the reality of littleness is sometimes called the *anawim*, or minority. This quality of evangelical littleness is like a jeweled light permeating the spirit and life of penitents. Spiritual poorness is understood as the central ideal of lay penitential spirituality: *"blessed are the poor in spirit, for theirs is the Kingdom of Heaven"* (Matthew 5:1). Minority or evangelical littleness can be defined as, **the blend of humility and simplicity, the fruit of being poor.** This spirit or quality is evident in the practice of contemplation, the relational patterns, the piety, and the mission of a group who view themselves as servants of mercy. All of the lesser brothers and sisters, as servants of love and mercy, do not expect to be thanked for doing what was commanded. *"So you also, when you have done all that you were ordered to do, say, we are worthless and useless servants; we have done only what we ought to have done"* (Luke 17:10). Therefore, in the words of Francis of Assisi, "humbly ask and beg all those who wish to serve the Lord God . . . to persevere in the true faith and penance.[53] Thus for penitents of love serving the Lord, minority or evangelical littleness expressed through servanthood is essential in order to know and love Jesus and our brothers and sisters with a personal love and a vital faith. Charity is resplendent in minority hearts full of mercy, expressed by those who are penitent servants of mercy.

---

53   Ibid., Earlier Rule

Chapter Four
Fruitfulness in the Penitential Life

The penitent's bond in the New Covenant love expresses a special charism which identifies one with the crucified Christ. This identification channels the graces of Crucified Mercy. Namely, that the Father of Mercies has generously bestowed on us the riches of His glory in His Son, the Incarnate Word made flesh. The Father of Mercies has poured out on us his benefits in true and holy love. The power of the Passion of Christ is the unique penitential charism, which enables penitents to surrender themselves in a process of conversion, which completes one in Christ with overflowing gratitude, glory, and praise. This unique gift enables the penitent to desire above all things to have the Spirit of the Lord working within his or her life. Therefore, penitents of mercy center on and in the Heart of Christ which provides the special way in which a penitent receives the necessary graces in one's life, relationships, and among the poor they live and serve. They freely choose **to drink the cup of suffering and to lead lives of life-giving repentance, conversion, and penance.** In this manner of living, one will advance the glory of God and be fruitful agents of his mercy as poor and humble penitents, freely choosing to live a penitential life by doing penance.

"I urge you therefore, brothers and sisters, by the mercies of God, to offer your bodies as a living sacrifice, holy and pleasing to God your spiritual worship. Do not conform yourself to this age but be transformed by the renewal of your mind, that you may discern what is the will of God, what is good, and pleasing and perfect" (Rom. 12:1-3).

The penitential life is certainly rooted in the soil of the Gospel. All good and every gift comes from above, coming down from the Father of Lights. He willed to give us birth so that we may be the first fruits of His creatures. The penitent experiences sometimes bitter, sometimes sweet cleansing mercy of the Lord. "Who is like you, the God who removes guilt and shame, and pardons sin for the remnant of His inheritance; who does not persist in anger forever, but delights rather in clemency, and will again have compassion on us treading underfoot our guilt" (Micah 7:18-19a). This concept of feeling shame is included in the biblical notion of guilt. Modern psychology tends to separate the two concepts of shame and guilt, into two separate entities for the purpose of clarity of understanding. This is believed to be effective for the counselee's ability to bring about change in one's life.

The penitential charism may be visibly present at the very beginning of one's conversion, growth, or reconversion. In fact in a certain sense one may say that it can even antedate an individual's recognized conversion. Some Christians already have accomplished prayer and penance before they experienced a specific call to become a penitent. Also the Holy Spirit may have given an individual significant grace that moves a person toward a more formal or concentrated effort to live the penitential life. St. Francis of Assisi arrived at a definite point in his early conversion through prayer and penance when he concretely recognized a call to do penance. Clare lived a penitential life as a little girl under the guidance and influence of her mother before she went through a special conversion with Francis. Francis then shaped his fraternity through a process of evangelical conversion.

It is well worth noting here that the process of conversion under the impetus of the penitential charism can take various shapes individually and collectively in a group's life, and then look very different at various stages of growth in one's life. Therefore, in determining our own **"wineskins" of being a penitent and doing penance,** both personally and communally, we need to look at the grace we are receiving. The charism and the anointing of the penitential call are significantly determined by our vocation, state of life, and the situation of the culture we are part of. The local church that we are a part of also determines some of our missionary activity. It is helpful for us to know what the need is in the Church in which we choose to serve. It is necessary for us to respond to the grace of the Holy Spirit to live a life of evangelical conversion and penance, in order to bring forth the **fruits worthy of penance.**

Being fruitful absolutely depends on the indwelling of the divine life and its active presence in the soul, and our cooperation with it. Also this fruitfulness increases the quality and degree of this precious gift of grace. A life of penance does not depend on the will power of a person alone doing various penances, but primarily on the action and power of God showing his Mercy. A call to be a penitent is a graced-call of love that invites us to respond as generously as possible to the Lord's saving Mercy. It is from a heart- felt gratitude, not simply from our will or desire, we can say "yes" to lead a life of penance. It is a life lived in union with God and for others, totally forgetful of an inordinate preoccupation of self. Our perseverance in penance is centered in the renunciation of self, required by the gospel. Egoistic self-love is put to death as we surrender our lives to a loving Father and gradually return to him to receive the fullness of life with him forever.[54]Paramount

54   The Liturgy of the Hours, A Treatise on Death as a Blessing

is the goal of reforming our lives and having our hearts purified, as we long for and then move to God with our whole being by the unceasing renewal of our lives. We accomplish these objectives by living in the power of the Passion of Christ, responding to the call of conversion, and undertaking a mission of mercy to live in and follow the will of the Father and please him as we become completed in the image of his Son.

"Apart from me you can do nothing" (John 15:5). *"The Father is glorified by this that you bear much fruit and become my disciples"* (John 15:8). *"But we must always give thanks to God . . . because God chose you as the first fruits for salvation through sanctification by the Spirit and through belief in the truth"* (2 Thessians 2:13). Jesus expects a penitent servant of mercy to bear fruit for Him and His kingdom. It is the Holy Spirit within us which conforms us gradually to Christ and makes us fruitful. However, there is a process of purification and transformation which accompanies the development of a life of virtue for the penitent, *"and everyone that does bear fruit he prunes so that he bears more fruit."* (John 15: 2) *"Every good tree bears good fruit, but the bad tree bears bad fruit . . . thus you will know them by their fruits"* (Matthew 7:17-21). In cooperating with the grace of the Holy Spirit we develop virtues, attitudes which produce fruit in our personality and character. The power of grace working on our natural abilities and acquired skills brings forth fruit for the kingdom. *"For the grace of God has appeared bringing salvation to all. Training us to renounce impiety and worldly passions, and in the present age to live lives that are self-controlled, upright, and godly, while we wait for the blessed hope and the manifestation of the glory of our great God and Savior, Jesus Christ"* (Titus 2:11-14).

"His divine power has given us everything needed for a life and godliness, through the knowledge of him who called us by his own glory and goodness" (2 Peter 1:3). *"Make every effort to support*

by St. Ambrose, vol. IV, p. 497

your faith with goodness, and goodness with knowledge, and knowledge with self-control, and self-control with endurance, and endurance with godliness, and godliness with mutual affection, and mutual affection with love. For, if these things are yours and are increasing among you, they keep you from being ineffective and unfruitful in the knowledge of our Lord Jesus Christ" (2 Peter 1:5-8). The development of virtue is part of a life of penance for a penitent servant of mercy. The Word of God, Scripture, is the central method: Francis of Assisi in the Earlier Rule encourages his brothers to live in the Word of God. He encourages them to hear the word with a good and noble heart, and understand it and keep it, and, bear fruit with patience. *"Be patient therefore, brethren, until the coming of the Lord. See how the farmer waits for the precious fruit of the earth, being patient with it until it receives the early and late rains. You too must be patient. Make your hearts firm, because the coming of the Lord is at hand"* (James 5:7-8).

Chapter Five

The Penitents' Mission: Intercession, Atonement, and Works of Mercy

The preeminence of Christ in his person and work is beautifully presented in the following Christological hymn in Colossians, *"Christ the fullness of the Godhead and the fullness of all grace is preeminent: He is the firstborn from the dead and placed over the community, the church, which He had brought into being. Also He is the crown of the whole new creation, over all things, whose further role is to reconcile all things to God through Himself. He delivered us from the power of darkness and transferred us to the kingdom of His beloved Son, in whom we have redemption, the forgiveness of sins. For in Him all the fullness was pleased to dwell, and through Him to reconcile all things for Him, making peace by the blood of His Cross. He has reconciled in His fleshly body through His death you who once were alienated and hostile in mind because of evil deeds, to present you holy, without blemish, and irreproachable before him"* (Colossians 1:18-22).

St. Paul develops this theme further in the Second Letter to the Corinthians, wherein he states that he is motivated by love because Christ has died so that those who live might no longer live for themselves but for Him Who for their sake died and was raised. *"So whoever is in Christ is a new creation. And all this is from God, Who has reconciled us to Himself through Christ and given us the ministry of reconciliation, namely, God was reconciling the world to Himself in Christ, not counting their trespasses against them, and entrusting to us the message of reconciliation . . . Be reconciled to God, in order that we might become the righteousness of God in Christ"* (2 Corinthians 5:18-21).

"No greater love can be conceived than this, that You should purchase my salvation at the cost of Your life. Let me run to You, the spring, and drink the divine draught that You cause to pour forth for the thirsty, offering water from Your side opened by the spear. Whoever drinks of this becomes a fountain of water springing up to eternal life."[55] The Merciful Heart of Jesus becomes the focus and center of this gift of Divine Mercy to the modern world. When our hearts are pierced by flames of love, and transformed into His Heart, we will receive the power to embrace the mission of mercy the Lord asks of us. The Heart of Christ is mercy itself, the vessel of mercy, a sea of mercy flowing out upon the whole world. The Merciful Heart of Jesus, which is the very person of Jesus Christ, and is the foundation and the unifying element of all Divine Mercy in the world, and all unique and particular expressions of it. "O Blood and Water which gushed forth from the Heart of Jesus as a fountain of Mercy for us, I trust in you."[56] Penitent Servants of Mercy, disciples of a crucified Master, we should let Jesus form our hearts modeled after his wishes and likings, the truth of the Father's will, always with goodness and mercy.

The specific role of power-centered reparation and atonement is rooted in the reality of reconciliation. Reconciliation means **to reunite,** to bring back to friendship after estrangement.

55   *A commentary on the Song of Songs* by Gregory of Nyssa
56   *Diary of Sr. Faustina*, pp. 186-187

God's mercy on humankind in the modern world is a great divine gift. It is in this fact that reparation and atonement have their tremendous power and significance. Merciful penitents give a primary focus, as servants of mercy, on imploring God's mercy. In our current global desperation, and in the Church, Pope John Paul II exhorts us to proclaim God's mercy, practice mercy toward others, and implore God's mercy on the whole world. "It is necessary that everything I have said in the present document on mercy be continually changed and transformed into an ardent prayer: into a cry for mercy on man in the modern world."[57]

About ten years ago I was living and pastoring on a Native American Reservation in South Dakota. One of our younger Friars came out to spend a month with me. He was interested in doing ministry among Native Americans. One day after living there for several weeks, he came into the house very upset about the poverty, drugs, alcohol, and sometimes violence he had witnessed on the Reservation. While he was vehemently expressing his great concern in which he stated that something needs to be done to fix all these painful situations. I recalled to myself a recent situation in our cemetery when I served at the burial of three members of the same family from Minnesota, a mother, a daughter, and a 12-year-old son murdered by the daughter's boy-friend. I was overwhelmed as three undertakers lowered the three caskets in the graves at the same time, while the Native drums were playing. The scene still brings tears to my eyes when I recall the incident. When he finished speaking, I quietly but firmly told him that we didn't come here to fix everything; we came here to share and give our brothers and sisters abundant mercy."

To proclaim, obtain, and do God's mercy in various ways is the purpose of a penitent's way of life. We proclaim, teach, administer, and live mercy in order that God's infinite mercy may be known and accepted by all, that *"God may have mercy on all"* (Romans 11: 32) The Lord granted to Brother Francis the grace to begin to do penance by serving the lepers. While he was in sin, this practice seemed very bitter to him. However, the Lord led Francis among the lepers and he had mercy on them. What seemed bitter to him was changed into sweetness, and after that experience Francis **really left the world.** God's plan is to have mercy on all. It is revealed as the sum of the Gospel. It is His greatest attribute; it is His creative, redemptive, and sanctifying love poured out upon us as sinners. In the Lord's words to Sr. Faustina, "Speak to the world about mercy: Let all humankind recognize my unfathomable mercy. It is a sign for the end times; after it will come the day of justice. While there is still time, let them have recourse to the fount of mercy."[58]

Because Divine Mercy is the source of our salvation, Jesus asks us, penitent servants of mercy, to proclaim, teach, administer, and live mercy in order to call ourselves and others to conversion, and to trust in the Lord. It is God's mercy we are to obtain and proclaim. Receiving His mercy in a trusting faith, we can be channels of that mercy to those in need, radiating His mercy to the Church and world. For us it is in the penitential tradition as penitent servants of mercy, who know, love, and serve God through a conversion of heart. Evangelical conversion is the hallmark of being a merciful penitent who is a missionary disciple. In a renewed fidelity of spirit, we are to turn totally and continually to the Lord and to our brothers and sisters. To know God is to be open to true faith and to our loving, compassionate, and merciful God. Being one with God is only possible in Christ. Penitents of mercy are invited to love God by the total investment of self, the total emptying and handing over of self to God, and the total commitment of self to God's purposes.

---

58   *Diary of Sr. Faustina,* No. 848

Jesus taught His disciples to be obedient to God by going through the process of complete conversion. As penitent servants, this conversion is rooted in the charism of mercy and finds its fruitfulness in the flowering of abundant and fruitful love through Contemplation. As we experience this process of conversion the Lord fills us with the love and desire to give back love for Love. Our minds are enlightened and our hearts are moved by the action of the Holy Spirit within, as penitents, to do Spirit-filled intercession, reparation, and atonement as a mission of merciful love.

This on-going process of conversion and penance expresses itself in our lives as radical poorness and humble littleness. This attitude of healthy dependence and surrender to God is interiorized through contemplation. This biblical littleness is one thing necessary for entrance into the Kingdom as we enter through the conduit of living mercy. The adult experience of childlikeness is the joyful awareness that one has been loved and chosen, and is the object of the pure love and favor of God. Possessing this littleness is attained through total conversion. This change of mind and heart is the result of experiencing and knowing the God who is Mercy Incarnate and loves us in his beloved Son.

Jesus is the servant of God's Mercy sent into the world to show us how to be mercy. The fruits of the Spirit, especially gentleness, meekness, humility, compassion, peacefulness, patient suffering and single-heartedness are the salient features experienced by penitents of mercy. Our mission calls us to love God's created world, and to become channels of Mercy to it and in it. As efficacious penitents we bring the saving Good News to the poor, proclaiming true freedom to captives, giving sight to the blind, and setting the downtrodden free as we announce the Lord's merciful favor and grace.

As missionary disciples, accomplishing compassionate mercy, a key goal of the mission, Christ and the Spirit intercede for us (See Romans 8:26,34). *"Therefore Jesus also suffered outside the gate to consecrate the people by his own blood. Let us then go to him outside the camp, bearing the reproach that he bore"* (Hebrews 13:12-13).

Jesus Crucified Mercy, a victim of love, has ransomed us from the fear of death and the power of the devil (see Hebrews 2:14). He has paid the price. Consecrated by obedient suffering, He draws those who are consecrated in Him into union with Him. We are sanctified through appropriating the gift of saving Mercy, and by the practice of prayerful atonement we join with Jesus in reparation and atonement for sin.

The Mysteries of Jesus are not yet completely perfected and fulfilled in his Mystical Body. These mysteries have been completed in the person of the glorified Christ, but not in us who are His members. This is brought about first through the graces He has resolved to impart to us, and then through the works He wishes to accomplish in us through these mysteries. Christ is being brought to fulfillment, in a sense, through His Church, and all of us contribute to this fulfillment. Christ achieves this process of completing the fullness of His life in His followers, as we move to the fulfillment of all things at the time of his Second Coming.

Christ's merits are infinite, and penitent servants of mercy in union with Christ provide a storehouse of graces and merits which possess expiatory value, the opportunity for healing, and the overflowing grace-filled transformation for His disciples by their good works of penance. The primary way this happens is for individual Christians to offer the daily sacrifices of the fulfillment of the duties of their vocations and particular states of life. Contemplative prayer, living in the power of the Cross, and doing penance provides superabundance of graces for the Body of Christ. Each and every one in his own way, to the degree called and gifted by the Lord, takes on the ministry of reconciliation by offering the gift of self as an atoning gift of love-filled immolation in union with Jesus to expiate sin and fulfill infinite measures of merciful love through a humble ministry of charity. We do this ministry through a dynamic and proactive union with Jesus. Atonement, emphasizing the unifying aspect of reparation and expiation, is geared toward the act of repairing and healing. The compassionate love and mercy of penitents witness to the works and the fruits of unity.

When one is called to share in Christ's redeeming love, it means a willingness to participate in His sufferings. No one who is inordinately in love with himself is capable of loving God as an instrument of merciful love. It is important to realize that suffering in itself does not have redemptive value. In this sense human suffering is an evil, but when it is done in union with Christ's divine love, it is abundantly fruitful. The person who loves God is the one who has mortified his self-love for the sake of the immeasurable blessings of divine love. The person who generously decides to undertake a life of suffering freely for the sake of the love of God and others will receive powerful gifts of grace to bring them forgiveness, healing, and conversion. This person never seeks his own glory, but only the glory of God. This person never seeks his own will but only the will of the Father. The life of St. Maximillian Kolbe, the priest of Auschwitz, was that sort of a life.

Suffering is such a precious gift of love. To embrace a life of prayer and atonement as a way of life is accepting the invitation to become one with the sufferings of Jesus. Our sufferings offered in union with the Eucharistic Lord act as a plea for mercy on us and on the whole world. We all have pain and suffering, and therefore, we can offer our interior and exterior sufferings to the Lord in order that He may pour out His mercy on all. We stand with Mary and John, gazing on the face of Crucified Mercy, and join as one with him in his total self-immolation to the Father. In union with the crucified Lord we offer our own hearts in the Heart of Jesus to the Father, and become one with the heart of the Father. All suffering and pains are useful and precious in the eyes of God if offered to Him. When grace fires our hearts, it stirs up in us a true thirst for suffering to show to what extent we love our Heavenly Father; for it is only through suffering that we learn how to love. In suffering and in persecution we reach a high degree of sanctity and at the same time bring others to God. May our faithfulness in suffering and prayers draw down the Lord's abundant mercy.

We are united with those individuals in heaven and on earth who, interceding and practicing atonement (At-One-Ment), win pardon, conversion, and sanctification for all. Let our ardent desires of love unite with the Heart of Christ, and in the power of the Blood of Jesus come before the throne of mercy and grace with Jesus. His voice is always heard before the throne of the Father. "Let us fix our gaze on the blood of Christ, realizing how precious it is to his Father, since it was shed for our salvation and brought the grace of repentance to all the world."

In Luke's Gospel Jesus goes to Nazareth to begin his ministry, and he stands up and quotes the same passage one finds in Isaiah 61 in terms of universal restoration: *"The Spirit of the Lord is upon me, because he has anointed me to bring glad tidings to the poor. He has sent me to proclaim liberty to the captives and recovery of sight to the blind, to let the oppressed go free, and to proclaim a year acceptable to the Lord."* (Luke 4:18-19).

By the love, power, and fruit of the Passion of Jesus and the gift of his new life of Resurrection may the work of reparation and atonement be magnanimously accompanied by a heart full of Compassion, **"Compassion Evoking Love-Power:" (CELP).** This approach increases a person's fruitfulness, and leads one to the practice of divine immolation which is a necessary completion to the gift of compassion and a life of prayer (contemplation). Let us fill up in ourselves those things that are wanting in the sufferings of Christ for the conversion of sinners, and by sacrifice, in union with Him, and without reserve be a gift of love. Reparation and atonement are not just ways of life but a complete life-style for those who prayerfully and freely choose to be penitent servants of mercy and missionary disciples.

Divine Love: The Ultimate Center of Life

No one can presume to take over our deepest and most personal desire and our heart's concern; intimate divine Love is the ultimate center of our life. In this reality we experience the freedom of being victims of love and missionaries of atonement in union with our beloved Lord, Crucified Mercy. Each day we invoke the power and anointing of the Holy Spirit to make this interior freedom possible. In the infinite dignity of the Father's merciful love in union with Jesus, we offer our gifted infusion of love, as victims of love in atonement and reparation for all as a vital means of personal transformation in ourselves, the Church, and the world.

Appendix I:

Merciful Penitent Fellowship Groups:

One may have had the opportunity to experience some spiritual renewal event over the years, and have been consistently faithful to their church commitments. And yet many still feel there is something more the Lord is asking of them as they desire to grow in holiness and give more of themselves to the mission of mercy. They may want to experience the joy of serving the grace of the Gospel together with others. And if they are looking for more opportunities for spiritual growth, human development, and fellowship than exists in their current situation, they may find other opportunities by participating in a **Merciful Penitent or Christian fellowship group.** The first steps in this direction would be to talk with someone about this desire, and then to seek out what is possible. Of course, the immediate question would be what is a Fellowship Group? First let me try to be clear about these matters about growth in the life of a penitent. This reality is fully available for any individual in any practical situation of life. In my travels over the last five years I have met many individuals who are already living a rich penitential life in their present circumstances. However, many individuals realize that some type of a relational format could be very helpful to them to make it more fruitful if they were doing this with others. It is also feasible to use the tools of modern technology to develop opportunities for communication: podcasts, emails, Facebook and other means of communications as well. This would obviously take some effort for those who are interested in working together to get some of these possibilities to happen. I would be willing to assist through my book and the subsequent podcast, noted at the end of this book, for anyone who is interested. The evils of the present time call us more than ever to be merciful penitents in service to the Lord.

It can become a challenging and frightening thing to read about all the Old Testament prophets, and what they say the Lord will do if the people do not repent and change their ways. And many passages in the Old Testament identify what God did do when the people abandon him and did not repent for national, communal, and personal infidelity. In three of the four Gospels, in the spirit of John the Baptist, Jesus starts his mission by calling the people to repentance for their sins. Yet today we are silenced by the false idols of tolerance, political correctness, rejection, violence, and many other inordinate fears which hinder Christians from boldly standing up for the truth that sets us free.

Scripture shows us that sometimes God himself imposes penances on the guilty - some sort of labor or adversity, often connected to the natural consequences of the sin. For example, the disobedient Israelite people are forced to wander in the desert for forty years because they would not go into the Promised Land when He commanded it (see Numbers 14:26-35). When a people excuse sin without repentance privately and communally, they extinguish God's light and are led into a disintegrating spiritual darkness with all its drastic consequences. Thus the Lord in his Mercy leads some servants of his mercy to inaugurate a response of love-filled atonement, life giving repentance, compassionate reparation, and merciful forgiveness with grace-filled healing; in other words, living a life of penance.

What do we mean by penance? Many of us know well the story of King David's sin with Bathsheba. Through the prophet Nathan, God confronts David over grave sins: adultery and murder. The guilty sovereign responds by confessing his sin to the prophet and to God. Then he humbles himself by exchanging his royal raiment for humble sackcloth, in hopes that the child born from him and Bathsheba, who was gravely ill, would be spared from death; and for a week he lies on the ground and refuses all food. David is performing self-imposed penance in his deep grief for his wrongdoing. His attitude and behavior illustrate how genuine penance includes both interior and exterior aspects. Interior penance is conversion of heart, a turning away from sin and toward God. It involves the penitent's intention to change his life because he hopes in God's mercy. We see David's change of heart reflected in his prayer of repentance on this occasion, recorded in Psalm 51.

External acts of penance include such actions as fasting, prayer, giving to those in need and other similar practices. These behaviors can have several purposes: demonstrating the penitent's intention to change; detaching him from the things he loves too much; drawing him closer to God; repairing some of the damage caused by personal sin, and participating in the reparation and atonement to God (satisfaction) made by Christ through His death on the Cross and His Resurrection to new life.

In some Christian circles today, when the word **penance or doing penance** is mentioned, one may experience a negative reaction. There appears to be a current resistive mindset among some sincere Christians against the practice of doing penance or the mission of intercession, reparation, and atonement. Is it possible that in our past there has been an overemphasis on the external aspect of practicing or doing penance? Or is it also possible that in our modern life we gradually have slipped into a significant disconnect in our penitential life from a deep interior enlightened life of grace and faith? Therefore, some of the ideas that have a negative ring actually have a rich and profound meaning for our spiritual life when they are connected to the interior life of grace and the work of the mission.

There are two major concepts which are united and operate in the dynamic experience of transforming grace in our lives; two sides of the same coin, so to speak. The first is our deepest aspiration to be united with Jesus, and serve Him as **missionary disciples of prayer, intercession and atonement in union with Jesus to the Father;** and the second is also being united with Jesus in the offering of one's life as a ransom for many, the gift of his love-filled salvation for all humanity. Both of these life-giving realities are intimately entwined through our dynamic participation and union with our glorified Lord, together fulfilling Jesus' mission in the establishment of the Kingdom of God on earth.

In the Gospel story in Matthew, Jesus calls the twelve together to explain the huge difference between the authority of those leaders in the world and those who lead in the Kingdom. He clearly states that those who wish to be great among the members of the community are called to be servants. Jesus points out that he came not to be served but to serve, and to give his life as a ransom for many (see Matthew 20:28). Therefore, the two notions of atonement to the Father and ransom of the many become one dynamic reality in serving the building of the Kingdom in our union with Jesus. This truth is the foundation of our merciful penitential evangelical life. In the same dynamic movement in which Jesus offers, consecrates, and sacrifices Himself to the Father, the Father accepts, receives, transfigures, and glorifies Him. Therefore, the painful and difficult experiences of life become a process of transfiguration.[59]

We need to join in a sacrificial union with Jesus and become a life-giver with and in Him. This means that we intimately enter into a union with the glorified Lord which profoundly realizes what it means to be a human being. We can only be fully human by fully entering into the divine reality of the glorified Savior. Thus, just as the seed falls to the ground and dies, we bear abundant fruit by dying to self, practicing self-renunciation and penance, and we are transformed in our movement to the Father. We actualize our humanness and self-transcendence in everything that we think, say, and do, and the Father lovingly accepts all we offer, large and small.[60] St. Paul's alerts us to this truth when he states, *"Always carrying about the dying of Jesus, so that the life of Jesus may also be manifested in our body. For we who live are constantly being given up to death for the sake of Jesus, so that the life of Jesus may be manifested in our mortal flesh"* (2 Corinthians 4:10-11). In the Mystery of Christ, we constantly experience His Death and Resurrection, which is our participation in the Paschal Mystery. All that we suffer and all that we offer to God are actually the hidden dimensions of the fullness of glory. The dying to self and all that we offer as merciful penitents is the gradual revelation of the Resurrection power and life in union with the Son of the Father.

Christian fellowship groups could be a context in which a person may receive an invitation to fellowship with **penitents of mercy;** those who are growing as missionary disciples on mission. Their humble service brings glory and atonement to God by living a penitential life according to the Gospel, doing penance and serving as a source of divine healing and

---

59   From a letter to the Corinthians by Clement, Pope, Liturgy of the Hours, vol. 111, 12th week in O.T., pp. 1513-1515
60   *Meditation in Magnificat,* July 2017, pg. 365, by Sr. Ruth Burrows, OCD

forgiveness for others. The God of infinite love dwells in the hearts and lives of those living in grace. A positive and abundant experience of God's love is a true path in daily sanctification and spiritual growth. The power of divine love is a wonderful incentive to grow in openness of heart to ascending degrees of Divine love.[61]   Gradually, with the grace of the Holy Spirit, one grows in holiness by sharing in the mystery of the Cross, which transforms difficulties and sufferings into an offering of love. The context of this transformation is a relationship in the power and life of the Glorified Risen One. This dynamic truth results in a life filled with the energy of divine love which enables one to choose daily "to pay back love for Love. Therefore, in union with Jesus who is Crucified Mercy, one exercises the gift of being a **victim of divine love.** From this truth the ministry and mission of atonement, reparation, and intercession is derived. This intimate personal divine love at the center of our life is what makes interior spiritual freedom possible. As we offer our experience as victims of divine love as gift, we personally engage in a vital means of transforming ourselves, the Church and the world in which we live.

---

61   Ibid., pp. 365-366

Appendix II:
Retreats and Designs for Grace of the Renewal Programs

Those who are interested or may want to affiliate with the penitential movement in the Church are rightly searching for the means of experiencing the necessary graces and the spiritual freedom, given by God to live this challenging and joyful evangelical way of life. Those who seek freedom from, are wearied by, and dissatisfied with living in the midst of the powerful cultural currents of radical secularism, and who desire something that is better than these negative forces of the "spirit of the world," deserve to be served in this quest for true freedom and a meaningful life. It is the Church's responsibility to provide the apostolates which will enhance these liberating opportunities for sanctification. The hidden mystery of the Lord's graces working in many who are thirsty and hungry for Christian holiness, or a better way of living one's human existence, needs to be complemented by the humble assistance of others who have made this journey themselves, and have the knowledge and experience to serve in this way. Therefore, some means of preparation is necessary for an individual to receive the maximum benefit of the **Church's Grace of the Renewal.**

Some who are searching are really ready, but our experience indicates that not everyone is ready. Therefore, it is helpful if there are welcoming opportunities for exposure to this manner of life, and to seek an understanding of what it means to be a penitent in today's modern society. This is one of the objectives of the podcast, along with the opportunity to work together to develop relationships and sharing with one another. Therefore, a basic and clear introductory preparation program to achieve the necessary openness to receive this life-changing grace would be useful. The goal of a preparation program, from a practical point of view, is to know what the **Grace of the Renewal** is, to understand it, to experience it, and then to live it and share it with others.

In recent times, as always in Church history, a powerful grace is at work in various ways in the renewal and reform of Church life. There are multiple expressions of this grace, and many have received spiritual benefit from them. The one I am most familiar with is the transforming grace of renewal, which is received by those who are in the Charismatic Renewal. Some of the early and youthful leaders who experienced this grace were wondering what to call it. The reputable theologians who were consulted suggested that it be called "the baptism in the Holy Spirit." The power of this actual grace has made a significant difference in the lives of many individuals and various works and ministries in the life of the Church over the last fifty years. The major tool used to prepare people to receive this grace is called **a Life in the Spirit Seminar.** The main gift of this grace, accompanied by various spiritual gifts, was brought about by an anointing of the Spirit, which resulted in a deep and lasting change in one's Christian life. An anointing could be defined as an infusion of the power of the Holy Spirit which makes the practical daily activities of a Christian's life grow in significant and life-changing ways.

However, since time has gone by, it has also become evident that the Holy Spirit is working in many people in a special manner beyond the confines of the Charismatic Renewal. It seems important to assist these individuals who want to experience a change in their lives, which is just as profound, yet may be more expanded than what has been experienced in their lives up to this time. This is the position that the reflections in this book have taken. The name which I have used to identify this preparation is the **Church's Grace of the Renewal.**

So therefore, what type of preparation and what should be the nature of the content of such a preparation? Without losing anything of the power and effects of the baptism of the Holy Spirit, is it possible to relate more directly to the power of the Cross and the power of the new life of the Resurrection in this endeavor? In addition to this approach, could the power of the Holy Spirit, the transforming power of the Cross, and the glorified power of the Resurrection become one unified life-changing experience? Could we call this **The Baptism in the Spirit of the Paschal Mystery Seminar,** which would include the power of Jesus Crucified, the power of the new life of the Resurrection, and baptism in the Holy Spirit? Of course, there would need to be a seminar or weekend retreat where the format, content, and preparation for this engaging and refreshing experience could take place. The scripture that most comes to mind in regard to this possibility is the Easter Sunday night appearance of Jesus in the midst of the disciples recounted in St. John's Gospel (see John 20:19-23).

Jesus appears in their midst and he proclaims, "Shalom!" (**"Peace be with you"**) This is the life-changing peace in which Jesus is announcing and proclaiming that He has completed the full expiation; through His gift of sacrificial love and atonement to the Father. Then He shows them His glorified wounds, and repeats His exhortation, adding, *"As the Father has sent me, so I send you." Immediately he breathed on them and said to them, "Receive the Holy Spirit. Whose sins you forgive are forgiven them, and whose sins you retain are retained"* (John 20:19-23). In this instant, they are anointed and commissioned: the glorified wounds, the power of the Cross, the power of the risen life, and the anointing of the Holy Spirit become one. Not only are they directly connected to the power of the glorified risen Lord, but also the power of the Cross and the power of the Spirit which becomes one reality! And they now have the authority to do what He did and will do again through them, an all-embracive evangelical approach to the mission and ministry of building up the Kingdom of God on earth.

The following outline is an attempt to tackle the unification issue of the threefold power of the Cross, the Resurrection, and the Spirit, identified in this work as the **Church's Grace of the Renewal.** Right from the start I would like to point out that there is a creative flexibility in this matter. There are many individuals and groups in the life of the Church who are very gifted in designing spiritual and pastoral renewal programs. I would invite them to take initiative in drawing up some possibilities for those who are seeking enlightened understanding and the freedom of the truth. This contribution could very well be a huge step forward in providing a rich new life in the Church's renewal.

The following is a list of themes which could be helpful for us to learn in order to move forward:

1. To look at what is happening in the hearts of individuals, and then focus on who is the person of Jesus Christ for them. What is the condition of a personal relationship with Him? How can one experience the power, glory, and wisdom of the Cross won for us by the sacrificial love and atoning death of Jesus Crucified?

2. To consider the three features and empowerment of the Paschal Mystery necessary for us to experience the new risen life of the glorified Christ. Then it would be helpful to look at all that it means to receive the empowerment and the anointing love of the Holy Spirit. This would be the time to pray with others to receive the actualizing Church's Grace of the Renewal, and the release of the fresh gift of the Holy Spirit in our personal lives.

3. To identify, acquire, and use the tools necessary to protect the graces we have received, and learn some of the things which will help us grow in the penitent life. For example, frequent personal prayer time, a spiritual growth plan etc.

4. The bestowal of special gifts: our natural an acquired gifts and interests. This would be the place to learn about the spiritual gifts and how they may be applied in our lives as well. Shifting our focus to service, we would need to have preparation and training in faith sharing, the skills of good communication, and specific methods of engaging in personal evangelization.

5. To consider various aspects of ministry and receive help in learning to pray with others, as well as the "dos and don'ts" of various ministries, for example praying with others for their specific needs.

6. The value of small fellowship groups which could meet for prayer, support, and various types of formation and training to serve, and encourage participants to generously return love for Love by engaging in some form of mercy work or other types of service.

Upon reflecting on the overall value of this work, one thing stands out with astounding clarity: living our journey as a pilgrim penitent of mercy can only be accomplished by a tremendous outpouring of God's love and grace. A noble and humble response on our part is only possible by a generous decision to gradually and peacefully surrender everything in our lives to a loving and merciful God, and together with others, embrace the vision of becoming a merciful penitent and a missionary disciple in the world and church in which we live. For reflecting further on the themes of this book, and the expansion and development of other related topics you may contact the podcast at **EvangelizingCatholicCulturepodcast.com**, or google **EvangelizingCatholicCulture.com.**

For the blessed grace to fruitfully continue to serve the Lord as his servants and disciples, using the prayer of enlightenment of St. Francis of Assisi, we pray:

Prayer for Enlightenment

Almighty, eternal, just and merciful God, grant us in our misery the grace to do for You alone what we know You want us to do, and to always desire what pleases You. Thus inwardly cleansed, interiorly enlightened, and inflamed by the fire of the Holy Spirit, may we be able to follow in the footprints of Your beloved Son, our Lord Jesus Christ. And by Your grace alone, may we make our way to You, Most High, Who live and rule in perfect Trinity and simple Unity, and are glorified God, all powerful forever and ever. Amen.

Acknowledgements

This book has come to completion through a huge number of communications over the internet and telephone with Felice Gerwitz, publisher and podcaster. She generously and capably guided me in the completion of this work. Her professional abilities and knowledge in the domain of publishing, author, educator, and podcast founder are the credentials she brings to her vision for Christian ministry. I have enjoyed and appreciated working with her to bring this project to completion.

Along with Felice I would be amiss if I did not thank Fr. Daniel Sinisi, tor, who checked the book for any theological errors, and gave to me many suggestions for improvement of the text. And finally, gratitude is very necessary to my Sister, Ruthayn Tickerhoof, who spent many hours with me on revisions.

Permission for the publication of this book was given by our present Provincial of the Sacred Heart Province of the Third Order Regular, Very Reverend Malachi Van Tassell, tor.

Notes

Notes

Notes

Notes

Notes

Notes

Notes

Notes